On Behalf of the Crazies

Sinéad Nelson

To Melissa,
  Thank you for supporting
  me and my writing!

  Love,
     Sinéad

For Bernie

I don't know where I would be without your compassion and support.

Thank you for getting me out of the Five Lamps, and giving me the chance to get my life back on track.

Table of Contents

When you tell your story, you free yourself
and give other people permission to acknowledge their own story.

—Iyanla Vanzant

Q&A, Minus the As

Deep down—and I mean *deep* down—I'm a bit of a nerd. Not in the sense of being really good at STEM subjects, owning a pocket protector, or rocking Coke bottle glasses. I'm talking about a particular delight I find in data. I'm a big fan of infographics, charts, trends, and statistics. I like facts and objectivity, and I like to understand what's going on and why things are happening. When things go sideways, I turn to research. I want answers. Factual, science-backed, empirically researched answers.

That desire for clarity and understanding is just one teeny tiny part of what makes mental illness so damn frustrating. Sure, there's research. Plenty of it, in an ever-growing collection. But it doesn't exactly tell you what's going on or what to expect. It doesn't tell you what people have experienced. It may give you the science of leavening agents but doesn't tell you what your loaf of quarantine banana bread will taste like. It can give you the science of neurology but doesn't tell you what to do about that one random Tuesday afternoon you'll have after months of remission when you just can't bring yourself to get out of bed.

And as the saying goes…if you can't find the book you want to read, you write it. Actually I don't think that's a real saying, but I needed a transition so just let me have this one.

Here's the thing: I'm not the only one in this situation. Far from it, actually. According to NIMH, nearly 20% of American adults live with mental illness. Research suggests that more than 16 million American adults have at least one major depressive episode in any given year[1]. There are millions of us nutters, each with crippling similarities and devastating differences. I haven't met all the crazies, but on behalf of the ones I have met…we want answers. We want to understand what we're facing on a day-to-day level, not on a theoretical neurological level.

I'm a few years into my second episode of major recurrent depression, and I want some answers. Some of my questions are new, and some are the same questions I've had since the beginning of my first episode nearly a decade ago. I want to understand what's going on in my brain[2]. I want to know when a sad feeling is just a regular old sad feeling, or when it's the start of another episode. I want to know how to tell people that my brain looks like one of those dozen-lane roundabouts in Europe that is flowing beautifully, but if even one car screws up a little bit, we're going to have a thirty-seven-car pile up, and that right now we're

---

[1] U.S. Department of Health and Human Services. (n.d.). *Major Depression*. National Institute of Mental Health. Retrieved September 27, 2021, from https://www.nimh.nih.gov/health/statistics/major-depression.

[2] Sidenote…if anyone has the connect for how I can get one of those brain scans, please hook me up. I want to see what's going on up there. I really, really, really, really want to know what I'm working with.

flowing well, but I don't know when one dumb little Prius is going to blow it for everyone. I want to know how to articulate what I'm feeling and what I need because right now I end up fumbling for the perfect word.

Those are my questions. That is what I want to know. I'm sure somebody out there has those answers, and it would be pretty rad if that person could share them with me. With every question I have, though, I also know that I have plenty of answers. I've made it through my near-decade of depression, and I'm still alive and kicking. As much as I want others to answer my questions, it felt right to add what I can to the library of experiences with mental illness.

The bottom line is that it sucks to be crazy. Nobody ever asks for mental illness. It sucks to have a broken brain. It sucks to know you're crazy and to have your craziness change from day to day, hour to hour, or even minute to minute. It sucks to feel like you're the only one with your particular, individual, unique blend of crazy. So, for all the crazies like me, I hope this book gives you a little understanding and a little less loneliness. And if you're reading this in the hopes of better understanding the crazy in your life, then on behalf of the crazies…thank you for caring, thank you for learning, and thank you for loving us despite it all.

Disclaimers

I am not a medical professional. I'm not even a medical amateur. I'm First Aid and CPR certified, I watch a lot of *Chicago Med*, I'm subscribed to Dr. Mike on YouTube, and I made it through a couple of episodes of *Grey's Anatomy* before I got bored, but that's where my medical training ends. There is nothing in this book that you should take as official medical advice. Literally nothing. You can take some of it and ask your doctor about it, but that's where my suggestion train reaches its final destination.

That's not to say I don't know what I'm talking about. I am absolutely an expert in my own stories and experiences. I did my research to make sure I wasn't just making up statistics or vaguely referring to things that have been disproven, but the bottom line is that mental illness looks different for everyone. Hell, it looks different in me from one day to the next. I'm not claiming to be a mental health expert; I'm claiming to be an expert on my experiences with mental illness. In a nutshell, please don't yell at me if Zoloft messes you up differently than it messed me up, and don't sue me if my pro tips don't work for you.

Disclaimer number two: I started putting trigger warnings where I thought they were necessary, and then quickly realized that this entire book is a big ol' pile of trigger warnings. This is a book about major recurrent depression and all the delights and devastations that entails. I'm going to talk about medications and coping strategies. I'm going to talk about suicide. I'm going to talk about my darkest moments. I'm going to talk about how it affected—and still affects—my family and friends. There are peaks among all those valleys, but if you're looking for a lighthearted book that focuses only on happiness, this is the wrong book for you. Writing this was a journey, and some of those valleys were incredibly difficult to relive; there are some passages that I even find triggering for myself, but I believe the value they add is well worth having to go back to that dark place in my memory. If it's too hard for you to read, just skip it. Nothing I write is so life-changing that it's worth triggering darkness or a negative spiral for you. Absolutely nothing.

Next disclaimer: I made up some people's names, partially for privacy's sake, and partially because I didn't know the legality of using doctors' and therapists' real names.

And finally, let's talk about the elephant in the room — well, the elephant on the cover. "Crazy." To many people, it's a regular old everyday word. To some people, it's an offhand reference to describe somebody who's a little off-center. And for others, it's a hurtful, offensive, derogatory term that serves little purpose beyond further stigmatizing mental health. When I chose to call this book "On Behalf of the Crazies," I knew the word I was choosing. I knew it wasn't a compliment, and that it is most often used with negative connotations. By definition, a "crazy" person is someone who is not mentally sound. I am not mentally sound. Therefore, I am a crazy person. A significant part of my work in therapy was coming to terms with that fact. I have worked hard to learn to embrace my self-proclaimed craziness, and doing so has allowed me to make significant progress in my recovery. It only seemed fitting that when I told my story, I did so with complete transparency and used the words that ran through my head every day. If it is a term you find unsettling or offending, I apologize for that. I suggest you swap it out with "People Who Are Battling Mental Illness But Are Still Human Beings With Depth Of Emotion And A Wide Range of Experiences And Should Be Treated As Such, Not Alienated For Their Differences," but all that didn't roll off the tongue as well.

Search History

Between August 31st, 2018, and May 31st, 2019, the first nine months of my second episode of major recurrent depression, I had more than 300 Google searches about depression, 85 about antidepressants in general, and at least 40 about the each of the antidepressants my doctors had me try. Most of the Google searches were about what I felt, trying to figure out if it was "normal." The rest were the questions I wanted factual, experiential answers for. Short answer: none of it was normal, but approximately a bazillion other people were going through the exact same things.

Even with all that googling, I couldn't find much on what I could realistically expect. All I had to go off of was the obscenely fast "Side effects may include this and this and this and this and blah blah blah" at the end of commercials on TV, and those are kinda terrifying. It's hard to take a whole lot of comfort in "you will most likely be less sad...but there is also a nonzero chance that you'll end up much sadder, your kidneys will spontaneously combust, you'll be dehydrated for four months, your head will never stop pounding, your heart rate will inexplicably skyrocket and plummet, and you'll hear a constant whistling in your ears." The lack of desired search results ultimately led me to write this book, but for those of you who don't feel like reading the next however many thousand words I wrote, I figured I'd just go through my search history and answer my own questions, rapid-fire style. Sort of like an FAQ, except it's only my questions and I only asked them once.

September/October

"Depression can't get out of bed"

Yup. Happens a lot. It's probably one of the hardest ones to explain—how hard could it be to sit up, put your feet on the ground, and stand up? Super hard, as it turns out. Because once you're up, the day keeps on going, and you have to keep producing energy and pushing through life. Staying in bed is safe and keeps the pain of the day to a relative minimum.

"Why does depression keep coming back?"

The answer to this one sucks. Depression is a chronic disease where the odds just keep getting worse; researchers have described it as a "highly recurrent" disorder. As noted in a literature review compiled by two clinical psychologists, once you've had a depressive episode, your odds of having a second one are somewhere around 50/50. Once you've had two episodes, your likelihood of a third is between 70 and 80%. After three, you're looking at a 90% chance of having a fourth. Studies conducted in the late 1990s suggested that people with a history of depression will have between five and nine separate depressive episodes in their lifetime[3].

"Depression worse in the morning"

Kinda the same as the "getting out of bed" issue. Morning marks the longest possible amount of time left in the day, and time is not your friend when every day hurts.

"Depression no appetite"

Loss of appetite is a symptom of depression and, when coupled with lack of energy, can end up with some pretty significant weight loss. I could count on having a bowl of Raisin Nut Bran most days, but there was little consistency beyond that.

"What triggers depression relapse?"

It could be nothing. It could be something huge. Both of my episodes were triggered by significant life changes—moving, starting a new school/career, and not being around people I know—but the trigger isn't the only thing going on. It took me a long time to differentiate a trigger from a cause. I visualized it as a breaking dam: the causes fill the dam with water, and those causes aren't necessarily choices or life events. They can be family history, past traumas, chemical imbalance, or so many other things. The trigger punches the first hole through the dam, ultimately starting the flood.

---

[3] Burcusa, Stephanie L, and William G Iacono. "Risk for recurrence in depression." Clinical psychology review vol. 27,8 (2007): 959-85. doi:10.1016/j.cpr.2007.02.005

"Does getting a pet help with depression?"

For me, yes. I was much better at regularly feeding my therapy hamster than regularly feeding myself.

"Depression feel like I can't breathe"

Turns out that was an anxiety attack, not depression. Whoops. Classic mental illness mix-up.

"Depression self-loathing"

Self-hatred can easily get mixed up with the guilt element of depression. It's hard to be the biggest fan of yourself when you hate your world and the pain you are inflicting on others in your world.

"Is depression genetic?"

Yes and no. There are some genes that Stanford nerds have connected to depression, but there are also a gazillion other environmental factors. The genetic factor appears to be negligible in my case, but I can't speak on behalf of all the crazies on this one.

"How to get through the day with depression?"

Million-dollar question alert! I guess the best I can say is to do what you're able to do, but don't push too hard. Accept that you are sick and that your mind/body is weaker than it used to be because of the disease. If you were recovering from a broken leg, you wouldn't decide one day that you're going to hop up and run a marathon. Your body can only take so much, and so can your brain.

"How to explain what depression feels like"

I wish I knew. Here are some beautiful quotes I've found that I feel like capture the essence pretty well:

"When you're depressed you don't control your thoughts, your thoughts control you." - Author Unknown

"A human being can survive almost anything, as long as she sees the end in sight. But depression is so insidious—and it compounds daily—making it impossible to ever see the end. That fog is like a cage without a key." - Elizabeth Wurtzel

"It is that absence of being able to envisage that you will ever be cheerful again. The absence of hope. That very deadened feeling, which is so very different from feeling sad. Sad hurts but it's a healthy feeling. It is a necessary thing to feel. Depression is very different." - J.K. Rowling

"I need help but don't want to talk to anybody"

I knew I was spiraling big time, and I knew I wouldn't be able to get myself out of the dark hole on my own. But I didn't want to see another therapist, I was scared to take medication, and I knew things would escalate if I mentioned it to my family. Bottom line, I knew I needed help, but I couldn't bring myself to utter the words.

"Depression medication risk"

This Google search came on the heels of my very first appointment with my regular doctor. I was terrified about all the side effects that came along with antidepressants. In hindsight, I'd like to pat myself on the back and say I was right to be scared about Zoloft, but in the moment, I was hoping Google would ease my worries at least a little bit.

Didn't happen. Side effects are whack, and it seems like everyone who has ever taken an antidepressant in the history of modern medicine has had a totally different experience. Google wasn't that helpful on this one.

At the end of October, I started my journey with antidepressants. My Google searches began to evolve in parallel to the adjustments to my meds.

November

"Depression quitting job"

I'm not sure why I googled this. Maybe to see if it was a common thing? Between the crippling depression compounded with the roller coaster of side effects, I didn't know how I was going to continue working. I was working retail at the time, and heading into the holiday season I honestly didn't know if I would be physically capable of showing up for my shifts and contributing at the level I expected of myself.

"How effective is Zoloft for depression?"

For me, not at all. It swapped out regular depression for supersize depression with a side of akathisia, so I'd call it a complete and utter failure.

"Depression don't want to get better"

It may seem senseless that someone struggling so much wouldn't want to get better, but it's a cornerstone of depression. I couldn't look forward to anything and truly didn't want to get better. I didn't want to take the meds and talk to therapists and grind through it all. I begged my family to let go and allow me to give up. The only comfort I felt was with my misery, and I wanted to bury myself in it.

"Depression physically hurts"

This was a weird one. My chest hurt, my back hurt, my feet hurt, and my head hurt. My heart was in physical pain, so I was trying to figure out if the meds were messing with my heart or if it was a depression thing, or if, on top of everything else, I was also going into heart failure at the ripe old age of twenty-four.

"What happens if a healthy person takes Zoloft?"

I thought I was being a baby. I was having a bad response to the Zoloft and feared that I wasn't depressed after all, and that's why I wasn't reacting well; maybe I was just a hypersensitive little pansy who couldn't handle being away from Mommy and Daddy and generally just sucked at being an adult.

December

"Zoloft makes me feel insane"

Turns out I was, in fact, kind of losing my mind. What I pegged as insanity was the early effects of akathisia. Point for me and my body awareness for recognizing that things were going sideways...but when I was just told to be patient and let things settle down and work themselves out, I lost that small victory. I'm still gonna go ahead and pat myself on the back for this one because I was bang on—Zoloft *was* making me feel insane!

15

"Zoloft rage"

I don't know to what extent my enraged feelings were caused by the Zoloft itself and its effects, versus how much was a reaction to losing my mind. Was Zoloft chemically creating the sense of rage in my brain, or was I enraged that Zoloft was making me feel extra crazy?

"Depression blaming parents"

I didn't blame my parents for much of my mental illness because I fundamentally understood that they couldn't possibly have caused it; however, when the meds were going completely haywire, I began to feel resentment towards them —Mom, in particular. It wasn't my choice to go on any sort of medication. I feared the side effects and had expressed that fear to my doctor at the first appointment. Mom felt strongly about it, so I agreed largely to appease her. Each morning when I woke up and took the pills I knew were making me feel even worse, I told myself that it was helping my family sleep easier, so it was worth it. On the flip side, though, when things went sideways, I was quick to place the blame on her. In my eyes, it was the definition of "I told you so." Everything I feared might happen was coming to fruition, but I just had to keep walking through the flames and hoping that at some point I would stop getting burned. I never felt actual hatred towards her, but whatever is a single step down from that is where I peaked. She was making me take the crazy pills, she was making me talk to doctors I didn't want to talk to, and she was the one who wouldn't let me give up—and I resented her for every one of those things.

"Brain scan depression"

I've said it before, and I'll say it again: I want a brain scan. I want to know what is going on in my head. I've seen the colored charts and diagrams highlighting brain function and how different parts of the brain show damage from mental illness. I want more than anything to see my brain. I plan on donating my brain to mental health research whenever I die, but I also want to know right now, while I'm still alive, what exactly is going on up in my attic.

"Depression chest pain"

Kind of an obvious one. My chest was hurting, and I didn't know why. I wanted to see if it was typical for depression or if my body was trying to end me through some cardiac issue. Turns out it's a pretty common depression thing, and that depression is one of the more common explanations for chest pain.

"Why is depression so hard at Christmas"

Holidays can be excruciating when you're depressed. On a regular day, people expect you to present as totally normal. They don't necessarily expect you to be skipping around in pure delight. On holidays, though, you're supposed to be extra happy…which makes battling a depressive episode on a holiday that much more challenging. For me, Christmas was the worst, in no small part because Christmas is my favorite holiday, bar none. My love language is gifts, so the entire Christmas season lends itself so beautifully to the way I show and receive love. I love Christmas Eve dinner, having cinnamon rolls on Christmas morning, helping my sister wrap gifts on Christmas morning[4], staying in pajamas, seeing my loved ones enjoy what I've so carefully selected for them…it's my favorite day of the year by a landslide. I put a tremendous amount of pressure on myself that I wouldn't let depression ruin the day for the family. At any cost, depression was not going to take away my favorite holiday.

When faced with truly life-and-death situations, the human body unleashes a near superhuman amount of power. You can find stories about people lifting cars, fighting polar bears, or treading water for hours to save loved ones, and it's because of this massive adrenaline boost—a boost you are physically incapable of recreating in normal circumstances— that allows their body to blow by every protective check and balance it has. The downfall of hysterical strength is the aftermath; when the adrenaline runs out, the crisis has been resolved, and your heart rate starts to settle, the consequences of using such hysterical strength come in. Overexertion injuries, like torn muscles and other sprains and strains, are typical results of hysterical strength. Your body can't normally access that much power, so your muscles aren't actually equipped to handle it. I think I was running on some small-scale hysterical emotional strength on Christmas. Desperate to make the day perfect, I pushed myself so hard to come across as happy and cheerful. By lunchtime, the hysterical Christmas spirit started to wean. By the evening, the consequences of my

---

[4] Nothing marks a procrastinator like wrapping gifts the day they're going to be opened. I don't think Brianna's gifts stay wrapped more than an hour, tops, before they get ripped into.

hysterical happiness came crashing in. And by the next day, I was in absolute shambles.

"Depression worse after Christmas"
Kind of the same answer as the last question: pushing so hard to make the day good, I completely burned myself out and needed time to recover.

"Depression living alone / depression move back home"
I lumped these two together because, even though they're technically separate search terms, they're two sides of the same coin. After Christmas, it was decided for me that living alone was not the healthiest or safest option at that time. I felt miserable regardless of where I was living, so I started looking to see if any research suggested living alone was better (or worse) than moving back home. There wasn't a whole lot of research leaning either way. In hindsight, moving home absolutely was the right decision, but at the time it felt like a walk of shame. In my eyes, I was moving home because I was incapable of being an adult and living on my own.

January
"Depression talking less"
When I'm around people I'm comfortable with, I won't shut up. I can be a complete chatterbox and talk your ear off, whether you like that or not. I'm an introvert, but if I'm in my comfort zone and we get onto a topic I'm passionate about, it's takeover time. By January, it had been a few months of dealing with the depressive episode, and I didn't feel like talking to anyone about darn near anything. Words felt like a waste of

time and energy, and I wanted to know if that was weird. Much like the chest pain question, it's a relatively common symptom. When there isn't much that you want to say, you aren't going to do much talking. Simple as that.

"Depression thinking is harder"

I searched this when I came across the "I feel stupid" roster of antidepressant side effects. I felt like my brain was moving slower, that I generally understood fewer things, that it took me longer to grasp concepts, and that there were far too many times that I completely zoned out of a conversation. Turns out, once again, it was pretty typical. Concentration, memory, and overall cognitive functions are often casualties of depression. It was validating to know that I wasn't just dumb as a bag of rocks, but I can't say I was crazy about how many different things I was googling and finding out were yet another symptom of depression.

"Depression decision making"

You'll never guess...but it turns out not being able to make a decision is also a symptom of depression! Three for three on symptom checks! On the scientific side, the difficulties in cognitive processing make it harder to evaluate options and make decisions. On the emotional side, it's simply because no choice seems like a good option. When you think about it, for every decision you make, you're just trying to pick the best option. Coffee or tea. Shorts or sweatpants. Salad or pizza. Call Grandma or text. Go to sleep or watch another episode of *The Great British Bake Off*.

When you're wearing depression-colored glasses, there

aren't any good options. Coffee or tea? It doesn't matter. Shorts or sweatpants? I don't care. Salad or pizza? I don't want to eat. Call grandma or text? I don't want to talk to anyone. Go to sleep or watch another episode? I don't want to be alive, so it does not matter. No option is a "good" option because, at the end of the day, I don't want to have to deal with any options.

"Thyroid and depression"

At my first appointment with a psychiatrist, I learned that depressive symptoms can at times be attributed to nothing more than a thyroid-related hormone imbalance. A family friend had helped Mom get me into a general practitioner quickly; so quickly that we blew right past the standard new patient onboarding protocol and fast-forwarded right to "Sinéad's depressed, let's get the meds going!" We didn't go through some of the standard procedures to rule out other potential causes of my depressive symptoms…like basic bloodwork. Once my psychiatrist realized those baselines hadn't been established, she scheduled me for a full workup. I pretended to understand what she was talking about regarding hormonal imbalances and thyroid issues, then went home and immediately started googling things. It gave me hope for a fleeting moment. Maybe my brain wasn't complete scrambled eggs. Maybe it was just a little thyroid situation that needed to get straightened out.

"Depression akathisia"

When I first saw the hourly rate for a psychiatrist, I thought I was getting robbed blind. I don't know of many other careers with a higher rate of dollars per minute. It's bananas. I quickly realized, though, that I wasn't just paying for her time in that moment. I was paying for the results of all her years of education and experience. Maybe ten minutes into the first appointment, after I had talked and cried through my feelings, my psychiatrist, Dr. Montez, had scheduled a complete blood panel, realized that I was dealing with some akathisia-type side effects, attributed those side effects to Zoloft, taken me off Zoloft altogether, increased the dosage of Wellbutrin, and modified the prescription to make it as cost-effective for me as possible. I darn near got whiplash from how quickly she moved to start getting things sorted out. If I had any complaints about her process, it would just be that she didn't really fill me in on some of the finer details of akathisia. I had trouble googling it because I had no clue how to spell it, but once I figured that out, I was off to the races[5]. In hindsight, I think it might have been intentional that she didn't tell me much about akathisia, otherwise known as "restless depression." Amidst all my personal chaos, I have a feeling she was trying to spare me from even more panic and worry about my mental and emotional state. It was good to have an explanation for why my body was spinning out of control, but it was also frustrating to know that I had won a bonus antidepressant side effect to go along with the standard ones. Much more to come on that, later!

---

[5] Sidenote: Do y'all remember in elementary school when you'd ask your teacher how to spell a word and they'd tell you to look it up in the dictionary? Why was that the response? If I can't spell the word, what makes you think I'm going to find it in the alphabetically ordered dictionary? If I happen to have the first couple of letters right, I might have a chance of finding it, but those nagging little silent letters at the beginning of the words? Or any words that aren't completely phonetic? How am I supposed to find any of those? I digress.

"Depression low white blood cell count"

In what was a surprise to approximately no one, we got the bloodwork back, and my thyroid was totally fine. Couldn't have been better. I have never been so disappointed to have a clean bill of hormonal health. I really thought that we'd found a loophole and that there could have been a possibility of a quick fix. But there wasn't. The only thing that stood out from the bloodwork was my notably low white blood cell count. That ended up being entirely unrelated to depression, but indicative of a weakened immune system. Nice.

"Depression avoiding family"

A thread woven through every depressive episode I've had is an internal conflict between leaning on family, while not wanting to bring pain to them. I know I need them. I know they are there to help me. I know they don't see me as a burden. But at the same time, I also know it isn't easy to support someone who's struggling. I know my thoughts, statements, and actions don't always line up, and if they do line up, they don't always make sense for the situation. I know it brings stress, sadness, pain, and anxiety into their lives, and that's the last thing I ever wanted to do. I'd rather stay home alone for days, crying and walking in circles and watching *The Great British Bake Off* on a loop than bring any more pain to my family. So, I tried to avoid them. I thought that maybe if they didn't see me in person, they wouldn't see how much I was struggling. If they didn't see my struggle, maybe they wouldn't be vicariously hurt by it.

February

"Pitied for depression"

Call it stigma, call it pity, call it misdirected compassion. No matter what label you put on it, it is easy for people to start looking at you differently when they find out you're fighting a mental illness. "Hey! How are you?" turns into "How *are* you?" with a weirdly intense look. If you tell them you're okay, they ask again with even more emphasis on the "are" part. I've always wondered what they're hoping to achieve with the repeat. I know for a fact that they don't actually want the entire internal monologue going on in my head; they may not know it, but if I actually shared everything, they would regret re-asking the question before I even finished my first sentence. If I turn "fine" into "actually terrible," then it begs a follow-up question that neither of us wants to deal with.

For someone trying desperately to stay strong and keep moving forward, few feelings can shatter you inside more than seeing pity in a loved one's eyes. When they look at you with pity in your eyes, you see them doubting your strength. You see them losing faith that you can get through this episode. You see them accepting the hopelessness of your situation and feeling bad for you that you're in such a hopeless position. As convoluted as it may be, since honesty is incredibly important in recovery, there are times that I need my support system to lie to me. I need some false confidence. I need some "fake it 'til you make it" energy.

"Wellbutrin side effects"

I think Wellbutrin (bupropion) is my favorite medication. It's a good one for me. It worked like a charm and was a knight in shining armor that saved me from the akathisia-riddled chaos that was Zoloft. But, as always, it was not without its side effects. The wildest one, and definitely least expected, was excessive sweating. After a ten-minute warm-up on the elliptical, you'd think I'd run a marathon across the Mojave. I bought special cooling towels because I thought maybe I was just running a little warm or working harder than normal. Not the case. After my extensive googling, I realized neither of those was the case. I was just a nasty little ball of sweat. There wasn't enough antiperspirant in the world to handle what my body was producing.

March

"Depression memory loss"

March was when I started to feel stupid. It was also when I started getting worried about how permanent some of the antidepressants' side effects might become. I couldn't count on my memory to do its job on a regular basis. After a particularly embarrassing moment when I couldn't find my way home from a grocery store that I'd been to a thousand times, inexplicably didn't believe the directions Siri was giving me and ended up calling dad to have him look up a map and tell me how to get home, I started to carry a small notepad around with me at all times. Anything I needed to remember, I wrote down. Anything I maybe, potentially, perhaps might have needed to remember at some point in the near or distant future, I wrote down. I wrote down tasks, recipes, to-do lists, directions, ideas, names, places, and anything in between. Was it overkill? Probably. But did it give me a small piece of control over my out-of-control memory? Absolutely.

"Wellbutrin memory loss"

The results of my previous googling weren't hugely inspiring or hugely helpful. They were the same results I'd seen months earlier, but I knew that what I was feeling was different. It wasn't the same cognitive sluggishness and general brain fogginess that had come solely from the depression when I wasn't on any medication. Unfortunately, this search was the first time I googled a symptom, and it didn't help. If anything, it made it worse. My newest medication was supposed to normalize cognitive function. It was not known to worsen memory; if anything, it was supposed to improve both verbal and nonverbal memory. And yet, there I was: black sheep of the crazies once again, defying what these medications were supposed to be doing.

"Depression forgetting words"

Verbal memory is wild. Absolutely bananas. I never knew it even existed until my brain went all mushy. My screwed-up verbal memory showed up in three main ways: forgetting words, losing information I'd heard, and the occasional Charlie Brown teacher noise. I've already talked a bit about forgetting words: mid-sentence, I'd lose a very basic word, not be able to find it (or a synonym), and end up with a train wreck of a sentence. Best case scenario, it was a group conversation, and someone else could pick up where I left off. Worst case, I was left with all eyes on me, producing toddler-level incomplete sentences. Losing information that I'd heard isn't that uncommon; it was just happening far too often. You know the feeling when someone is talking to you, and it goes in one ear and out the other? It was that feeling, multiple times a day. Sometimes, even multiple times in a single conversation. I was too embarrassed to keep asking for things to be repeated, so I'd take what had stuck, try to fill in the gaps with some context clues, and hope for the best. The weirdest verbal memory lapse, by far, was what I could only describe as the Charlie Brown teacher noise. If you don't know what I'm talking about, go ahead and look it up really quick. I'll pause here. There's a ten-second video on YouTube that is just the sound.

Alright, welcome back. So, the Charlie Brown teacher noise side effect. A whole bunch of "wah wah wah." I'll be talking to someone and mid-conversation, sometimes even mid-sentence, their words will turn into complete gobbledygook. It's a string of meaningless sounds. They aren't mixed up words or anything like that; it's verbal nonsense. A baby babbling, a tape recording playing backward, or a fictional foreign language. It sounds like Simlish. Or Elvish. Or Na'vi. Or Klingon. Or Pig Latin. It's a language I don't speak. Luckily, since whomever I'm talking to doesn't know that in my brain they've just switched into absolute nonsense, I can laugh and say that I zoned out, and ask them to repeat it. The second time through, it's usually fine. On the off chance that it isn't fine after the second go around, I go back to the aforementioned strategy of taking what I can get, filling in the gaps, and sending up a prayer that I don't irreparably screw anything up.

Episode One

April 2012 to March 2014

Running Away From Problems

I am a big fan of running away from my problems. I like to think of it as "creating space between you and the things that bring you undue challenge" because that makes it sound more official and less of a chicken move, but the bottom line is, I'm a runner. Is a conversation about to get awkward? End it. The person I don't like is on a direct route towards me in a room? Hide in the bathroom. An undiagnosed depressive episode is making college a tough transition? Drop out of school and flee the country.

In hindsight, was hoofing it to the other side of the world the best move? Probably not. But did everything happen for a reason to get me right here, where I'm now happy and fully employed and living a good life? God, I hope so.

et's take this all the way back to 2012. Senior year of high school. Good times all around. I drove a Suburban that could easily fit nine people, so any time my friends and I hung out we'd pile in the 'Burb and go make some memories. My class schedule was a delightful joke: Student Government, not advanced English; Yearbook, not advanced History; and home by lunchtime. Absolute serendipity. Senior year is a bizarre juxtaposition of feeling like you're on the brink of becoming an adult and making adult decisions, but also wondering who the hell thought you were ready to become an adult and make adult decisions. The biggest decision? College.

I had narrowed down my college choices to two: the University of Oregon and the University of Portland. My dream school, Gonzaga, had waitlisted me, and I was too proud to wait for their response. I was ready to make my final decision. In mid-March of 2012, Mom, Dad, and I took a weekend trip up north to visit the University of Portland and the University of Oregon. First was the University of Portland, a smaller private school with a legendary soccer program but no football team. My sister Brianna's best friend, Lauren, went to Portland, as did our next-door neighbor. We went to the standard welcome events in the morning and then had our own private, more insightful tour with the pair of them in the afternoon. By evening, when we headed to downtown Portland for dinner and ice cream, I was pretty convinced. The University of Portland was my place. It seemed comfortable and perfectly lovely. I remember telling Lauren that Portland would be it unless I fell in love with the University of Oregon.

Spoiler alert. I fell in love with Oregon—technically, before I'd even set foot on campus. As we drove into Eugene, I caught a glimpse of the massive "O" logo atop Autzen, the Oregon football stadium. I was sold. I told Mom we didn't even need to go on the tour. It was love at first sight. Mom made me go on the tour anyway, but everything became a self-fulfilling prophecy by that point. I found a silver lining for absolutely everything. The dorm rooms in Bean Hall are so small you can hold hands with your roommate while you sleep in your separate beds? Sounds like a great way to bond quickly. It rains 300 days out of the year? Fantastic, I love the rain! Nobody in the state of Oregon knows how to cook with spices bolder than salt and pepper, and you won't get good Mexican food anywhere? Wonderful, I'm a bland-food eater anyway. People make fun of Oregon for being the "University of Nike"? HA. Like that's even an insult. By the time we got back to the hotel room that night, I had already filled out my housing application and submitted my deposit. It was go-time. We flew home Sunday night, me proudly rocking my new Oregon hoodie (forest green sweater with yellow "Oregon" across the front—a timeless, classic design). When we got home, I looked through the mail that had been delivered over the weekend and found a letter from Gonzaga; I had been accepted. But it was too late. I was locked in on Oregon.

I rolled into school Monday morning feeling like an absolute legend—still proudly rocking my Oregon sweater as well as the Oregon women's basketball t-shirt we'd bought at the Duck Store. I couldn't wait to tell the world that I, Sinéad Nelson, was officially going to be an Oregon Duck. The reaction I got from everyone I told was pretty much identical, something to the effect of "Oregon is the perfect fit for you!" And on paper, it absolutely was. Close enough to home without being in my own backyard, a massive sports culture, and strong enough academically without being impossibly challenging. It *was* the perfect school for me.

As my last year of high school edged closer and closer to the finish line, I started to get a pit in my stomach that I had made the wrong choice. When I went back up to Oregon in early June for IntroDucktion (Oregon's version of orientation—Duck puns are in no short supply at that school), I called Mom incessantly to come to pick me up because I was so miserable. Some level of second-guessing is inevitable when it comes to a decision that big; it was the most important choice I'd made up to that point in my life, and I didn't know what the consequences could be if it proved to be the wrong choice. What felt especially wrong, though, was that I couldn't figure out the right choice. I didn't want to change my mind; I simply wanted to un-make up my mind.

Portland didn't seem any right-er. Gonzaga didn't seem right, either. Linfield, where I had an opportunity to play basketball for a coach I really liked, wasn't right. I was starting to think that it wasn't an Oregon problem. It was a college problem. There wasn't going to be a "right" school when the entire idea of going to university felt so inexplicably wrong. But I was Sinéad. I was a Nelson. I was the younger sister to Brianna, who was flourishing in her second year at UC San Diego. And I was going to college. There had never even been a discussion in our household about anything else. Over the summer, when I tried to tell Mom I didn't want to go, she shut me down faster than LimeWire on a Dell. I can't blame her for that. I didn't have the words to articulate why I was feeling that way, and even in my own mind, I wasn't sure what exactly I was feeling. All I knew was that something felt very wrong. If we had been in a movie, it would have been the time when sad music starts playing in a traditionally happy scene, just to let the viewers know that things were not peachy. But we weren't in a movie, I didn't have a soundtrack to set the tone, and things were expected to become peachy on their own.

It's worth noting that I had never been diagnosed with depression at that point. I had been diagnosed with PTSD a couple of years prior, and during that process, I was also tested for ADHD (which turned out to be anxiety...who knew?). We never thought to look in the good ol' DSM-IV[6] for an explanation, because mental illness wasn't on our radar at all. Mom thought I was just getting a head start on homesickness, and since I didn't have the verbiage to explain what I was feeling, we ended up stuck on that purely by default. We didn't talk much about college that summer; I knew in my gut that going off to school was not the right call, but Mom wasn't interested in replaying the same argument over and over. To be fair, she had history on her side.

One of the fundamental tenets of my personality is being bad at major life transitions. I have no memory of it, but I assume I did not enjoy leaving the womb and entering the world. Thankfully, I'm the youngest of the family, so I never had to adjust to a new sibling joining the crew. Pre-K to kindergarten was rough. Elementary to middle school was rough. Middle school to high school was rough. If prior experiences were any indication, it only made sense that high school to college would be equally rough. But I knew in my heart of hearts that what I was feeling was different. It wasn't just nervous adjustment energy—and I

---

[6] The Diagnostic and Statistical Manual of Mental Disorders, 4th edition. Basically an encyclopedia of all the different kinds of crazy, published by the American Psychiatric Association.

was very familiar with that energy—this was different. This was my own little Jiminy Cricket telling me things were not right. Jiminy provided an underwhelming amount of context or explanation, but he was getting the message across: things were not on track.

By the end of the summer, I still had no explanation for what I was feeling. I didn't even have a semblance of a solid reason why I shouldn't go to Oregon. I had run out of time to figure anything out, so I went. Dad and I packed up the truck, and we made the drive up I-5 to Eugene, Oregon. The knot in my stomach grew with every mile, and I was nauseous by the time we arrived.

I had early move-in because I had signed up for a two-day freshman-only leadership class before the term started. Dad got me moved in and stayed with me up until the meet-and-greet session for the class was about to begin. Free time has never been my best friend, especially in emotional situations, so he stuck around until the last possible second. Then he left me standing on the sidewalk, sobbing hysterically as he drove away. I don't know if I was trying to get an Oscar nomination or something, but it was the most dramatic moment I possibly could have created. His pickup truck driving into the distance as I stood alone on a sidewalk, silent tears streaming down my face…it was beautifully devastating.

I went to the meet-and-greet, met a few people, and got a cup of lemonade spilled in my lap. Good start. Nothing says, "welcome to college!" quite like looking like you peed yourself on day one. I then went back up to my bedroom to try to settle down, but my body didn't get that memo. Instead, my body got as unsettled as I'd ever been. I couldn't stop shaking and crying. My heart felt like it was going to explode, and there was absolutely nothing I could do to stop it. I could barely breathe, and it felt like the one time my cat fell asleep on my face and accidentally sort of suffocated me. It reinforced that I was right: something was very wrong, but I still didn't have the verbiage to articulate what was happening. I realized years later that that had been my first full-blown panic attack.

That was the first night that suicide ever crossed my mind…and if anything could be worse than a spontaneous panic attack, it's your own mind suggesting that maybe you should eat a bullet and try again in another life. The moment you realize you are no longer in control of your own thoughts is equal parts humbling and petrifying. But through it all, I still couldn't find the words to what I was feeling. I could have called Mom every hour on the hour for weeks, and never would have figured out how to explain it. Everyone told me it was normal to be nervous about adjusting, and blah blah blah. But I knew that wasn't what I was feeling. I'd been homesick before, I'd been in awkward transitional situations before, and I knew what those felt like. That wasn't what my gut was telling me this time around. My gut wasn't being super communicative, so I couldn't say what it was…but I knew precisely what it wasn't.

I couldn't eat much for the first few weeks; I'd go to the dining hall, buy some food with my meal points, eat maybe three bites, and toss the rest[7]. I'd put on my brave face when I met new people, then as soon as I could find somewhere I could be alone, I'd cry. There was a lovely balcony on the third floor of the

---

[7] I got my Freshman 15 a little backwards, and ended up losing 15 pounds in the first 10 weeks of the school year.

business school that overlooked some lawns and trees, which became one of my favorite reading/crying spots. I remember reading *Warriors Don't Cry* and feeling like a complete and utter baby; those children were tasked with being the guinea pigs of desegregation while I was just going to college, and yet our reactions were darn near identical. Their reactions were arguably more rational than mine. That's just plain embarrassing for me.

Truth be told, I wasn't even super clear on why I was crying. You know when you get hit in the face with a ball, and even if it doesn't hurt, your eyes start watering anyway and it looks like you're crying? It was sort of like that, minus the getting hit in the face, and instead of teary eyes it was actually crying. I didn't want to be at Oregon. I didn't want to be at home. I didn't want to be at Portland, Gonzaga, or anywhere else. I didn't want to be anywhere.

Looking back, it's crystal clear that I was at the tip of the iceberg of suicidal ideation, but at the time, I had no diagnosis or language to describe all that. I just knew that I felt bad all the time. I could set up an evening of complete bliss, curled up in my bed, on the phone with Mom or Brianna, eating a pint of Ben and Jerry's Milk and Cookies ice cream and watching Glee, and I'd still be miserable.

In the span of just a few weeks, I convinced myself that the problem was, in fact, Oregon. At the time, I was a pre-journalism major, though I had very little confidence in that decision. I thought I might want to be a teacher, but Oregon's education program was a four-year program, which still didn't give you a teaching credential upon completion. I also thought that maybe I wanted to do some sort of sport management, kinesiology, or coaching—more programs that Oregon didn't offer. In hindsight, these are the sorts of things I probably should have looked at before choosing a school, but that ship had sailed.

I thought getting farther from home be the right move. Maybe I could pack up, start a new life somewhere else, and leave my problems in Oregon. I considered the University of Florida, UConn, Syracuse, and Kansas, but those didn't seem like they'd be far enough away. If I was going to successfully run from my problems, I needed to be as far as humanly possible. Like, out-of-the-country far. My mom's side of the family is Irish; I'd been there many times and loved it—and I have dual citizenship. I also discovered that University College Cork (UCC) had a Sports Studies and Physical Education program. Bingo.

Mom was hesitant about the whole idea, but nonetheless helped me out with my application and rounding up the necessary letters of recommendation. I hadn't made much of a splash with any of my professors at Oregon, so I had to go back to high school teachers to get what I needed. I had moved up to Oregon in mid-September; by the end of September, I was determined to get out of there. By the time Mom visited in early October, I had downloaded the application for UCC. By Halloween, my application was submitted.

Through each step of the process, I continued convincing Mom (and myself) that I wasn't running *from* Oregon; rather, I was running *to* Cork. Regardless of how I creatively framed the situation, the bottom line is that I dropped out of Oregon after the first term. Ten weeks, and I was out of there. I was going to Ireland in the fall of 2013, and that's all anybody needed to know.

Unfortunately, when you come back from college empty-handed and about three-and-a-half years too early, there's a whole lot more that people want to know. I had a web of half-truths prepared: Oregon didn't have my major (mostly true, but I didn't exactly know my major yet); I was going to be going to school in Ireland the following fall, and the transfer credits wouldn't even count (factually accurate, but leaving out some details); I couldn't decide on my major and we didn't want to be wasting money on me taking general ed classes at Oregon (true that I couldn't decide on a major, not-so-true that it was a financial decision).

The thing I struggled with most of all, though, was that I didn't actually know the true answer. Even if I'd wanted to, I couldn't have told people what I was dealing with, simply because I didn't know what was going on in my head. I knew I was hurting, I knew I hated my life, I knew I hated myself, and I knew I was miserable every day—but we still hadn't pieced together that I was experiencing my first episode of what would become major recurrent depression.

Over the winter break, Mom and I went to Ireland to visit some family and take a good hard look at UCC. We toured the campus and the athletic facilities; it was a real possibility that I could have played basketball there, though "college sports" in Ireland are nothing compared to the madness stateside. I felt pretty good about it, but we held off on putting down deposits until we'd taken more time to let things settle—Mom was not about to let me make another trigger-happy mistake.

Back home, I went to a semester of community college, coached some youth soccer and basketball teams, helped out at my high school's dance show, and counted down the days until the end of the school year. By February, though, good ol' Jiminy told me that my new plan also wasn't the right one. So, I bailed on Cork. Bailed on school altogether and decided on a gap year—but still in Ireland. I remained confident that fleeing the country was the best plan of action. I signed up to work with a volunteer program designed to build faith, character, and self-esteem into the children they work with, all grounded through sports. Nothing would stop me from running to Ireland and leaving my problems in America.

Annoyingly (but entirely predictably), that's not exactly how mental illness works. The messed-up brain I had in California is the same messed-up brain I brought to Oregon and is the same messed-up brain I took across the pond. That was a real disappointment. Simply put, my stint in Ireland was nothing short of a fiasco and-a-half. I arrived on September 4th, and by September 13th, I was determined to run from there as well.

Running Into New Problems

If you're the superstitious type who believes in omens and whatnot, you would have foreseen from the very first moment of my voyage that I was destined for disaster. My flight from San Francisco to London was delayed, making my connection in Heathrow a real delight. If you've never been to Heathrow airport, consider yourself blessed. I ended up sprinting through the labyrinth that is Heathrow airport and made it to my Dublin connection by the skin of my teeth. I felt truly awful for the poor woman sitting next to me; I was dripping with sweat, panting, looking very disheveled—and I'm sure I smelled horrible.

Mercifully, it was a short flight. We landed in Dublin, and I headed to the luggage carousel, my stomach in knots. I thought a snack might settle my stomach, so I bought the plainest biscuits I could find in the vending machine. I ate half a biscuit, then proceeded to (literally and figuratively) toss my cookies in the nearest trash can. Once my bags came around, I dug out my toothbrush and tried to freshen up a little bit before the program coordinator, Dave, arrived to pick me up. I wasn't too concerned with the first impression, but I figured sweaty and vaguely vomit-scented wasn't ideal.

Dave took me to the "apartment" they had coordinated for me; "apartment" being a very generous description for where I was going to be living. I'd call it more like a studio, at most. A distinct lack of walls made it even more awkward when I discovered that a woman named Valerie already lived there. Dave had conveniently left that part out. As it turned out, that was the first of many things I would quickly discover that Dave had conveniently forgotten to mention. They actually didn't have any place for me to stay, but Valerie was a friend of Dave's and said I could crash with her. I know I wasn't in a position to be picky, but when I say this flat was awful, I really mean it. It was truly, wholeheartedly, horrific. I would have traded Harry Potter for his cupboard under the Dursleys' stairs in a heartbeat. Hell, I would have paid Harry to let me take his cupboard instead. The area had been described to me as "very near Dublin city centre," which was *technically* accurate. But that's like describing Compton as "very near Los Angeles." You're not wrong…but you're leaving out some very critical details.

The flat was in one of the worst areas in Dublin—the cross street was nicknamed Sheriff's Street because of the frequent—and highly necessary—law enforcement presence. I didn't have a room, because the only walls it had were a perimeter to the bathroom; the bathroom didn't have a door, so it's hard to give full credit on the walls. My bed was sandwiched between the radiator under the window (definitely a fire hazard) and the counter above the mini-fridge. The microwave sat on a precarious shelf above my head, and all the dishes were balanced Jenga-style atop the microwave. Thank the Lord we weren't in earthquake territory, or my head would have gone from 3D to 2D with the first tremble. My "closet" was a rickety wooden rack with a piece of canvas draped over it. I've seen popsicle stick towers with more structural integrity than my closet.

The flat was above a Chinese restaurant, and to get into the building, you had to use a key to open a metal shutter (not unlike the ones you see outside stores in areas of questionable security). Sirens blared past the window every night, and one evening as I was walking home, a police officer stopped me to confirm I knew where I was going. I guess he didn't believe me when I told him I was confident in my address. He triple-checked my address, looked me up and down, and decided he was going to walk with me right up to the front door—or, I guess, the front grate.

After a confusing, sleepless night, I headed off to work the next morning. I prayed that it would be a rewarding, energizing, refreshing validation of everything I'd gone through to get there. It wasn't. Not even close. Even if, by some miracle, my head had gotten itself in order overnight, work probably would have driven me to depression again on its own.

The volunteer program had been advertised as an organization that used sports—particularly basketball—to serve underprivileged kids in Ballymun, one of the roughest parts of Ireland. Crime rates were high, education rates were low, and average socioeconomic status was sub-basement[8]. The program's goal was twofold: first, to give the kids activities to get them off the streets and into a safe place with good role models; and second, to reinforce to the kids that they are wonderfully made and that they are perfect just as they are. I was wholeheartedly on board with both of those elements. There was an underlying theme of spirituality and biblical connections, but it wasn't a crazy religious program. On paper, everything sounded great.

In reality…not so great. About as non-great as you could get, really. There was no time spent on training or introductions, and the other volunteers and I were dumped right into working with the kids before we even knew each other's names. The directions I was given consisted of: take the bus out, and when you see the IKEA, get off at the next stop. Then walk quickly to the facility, so you can get through the door before anybody has time to bother you.

Three days into the program, it was starting to become crystal clear that things were not off to a good start and were highly unlikely to turn around. The trend that had been established with my flat—forgetting to mention critical pieces of information—ended up foreshadowing a vast majority of all the other issues. The program hadn't communicated their belief that the kids get nothing but discipline at school, so we should just let them go absolutely bonkers at basketball practice. Practice devolved into an hour of absolute chaos within the first five minutes. It wasn't even organized chaos; it was anarchy. One of my players decided she wanted to just roll on the floor, and I was

---

[8] Schiller, Robin. "Dublin City Had Highest Crime Rates in Ireland Last Year, New Figures Show." Sunday World, 5 Apr. 2021, https://www.sundayworld.com/crime/irish-crime/dublin-city-had-highest-crime-rates-in-ireland-last-year-new-figures-show-40274674.html.

instructed to ask her if she'd like to stop rolling on the floor, but if she didn't want to stop, I should let her keep rolling. She was eleven years old, rolling like a water bottle down a hill right across the gym floor. But we weren't supposed to critique anything about them, because they were "perfectly made just as they were." Call me crazy, but I feel like rolling on the ground while someone is trying to teach you something, or communicate with you at all, is something of an imperfection.

Beyond the complete lack of structure and support, what broke my heart the most was the fact that we were not actually working with the kids the program claimed to reach. Yes, the program was set up in a disadvantaged area; however, we were explicitly instructed not to let certain kids into the gym. There weren't any photos on the wall of specific children, but there might as well have been, with how small the community is and how boldly the lines had been drawn. There is a small population of native Irish people referred to as "Travellers." They are similar to what other cultures describe as "gypsies," but the Travellers are indigenous Irish[9]. Their hygiene isn't great, they can be a bit rough around the edges, their family structures aren't the most traditional, their health tends to be worse than most others, and their children are usually raised outside traditional educational systems. We were explicitly told not to allow any Traveller children into the gym, regardless of the circumstances. It was fall in Ireland, so it rained a lot. No exaggeration, we were instructed to lock the doors and leave those kids standing in the rain, their faces pressed up against the windows.

---

[9] Keefe, Alexa. "The Irish Travellers Uphold the Traditions of a Bygone World." Photography, National Geographic, 4 May 2021, https://www.nationalgeographic.com/photography/article/irish-travellers-uphold-the-traditions-of-a-bygone-world.

It broke my heart and made absolutely no sense to me. In my eyes, the Traveller children who just wanted to come to the center and play basketball should have been the ones we welcomed with open arms; instead, we turned them away. For a program that served disadvantaged youth, we were turning away a whole lot of very underprivileged kids. I understood that they would likely be a challenging group to work with, but we should have been walking the walk if that was the talk we were going to talk. If the program didn't actually want to work with those kids, it never should have been advertised as though it did.

One way that we kept the Travellers out of the program was by charging for each individual practice. Instead of setting a registration fee at the beginning of the season, the kids were charged every day. They'd show up at the gym with their €2, which allowed them entry to the practice. No money, no practice. Except for some nice kids who had been around for a while and were probably good for it. And except for a few other nice kids who the program director let slide. And except for a handful of kids that just marched in and grabbed a basketball, since we had no methods to discipline them and they knew they weren't going to get booted from the gym. It was the same policy for the Sunday youth club and the Saturday morning basketball clinics.

It was incredibly frustrating—in that part of the country, €2 is a lot, and would add up quickly. If a family had two kids each doing one practice, one youth club, and one clinic a week, they were looking at more than €80 for a single month. Take that out for the whole year, and you're looking at nearly €1000. That was doable for the relatively advantaged folks in the area, but was a significant barrier for the kids who really needed what we were doing. In essence, we helped the gentrified folks of Ballymun, while literally locking the doors on the genuinely disadvantaged.

I don't believe in letting kids wreak havoc during basketball practice and ruin the experience for the other players genuinely trying to get better. I don't believe in advertising a program to help disadvantaged kids that doesn't actually do so. I don't believe in leaving out bits of the truth to people who are flying around the world, leaving home for a year, and being paid nothing to work in your program. And, above all, I don't believe in what they ultimately ended up teaching the kids: no accountability for actions, no discipline, no motivation, and poor sportsmanship. Every day I went to work, I actively went against some of the core parts of my identity. That would have been tough to handle anytime, but the real cherry on top was that, through it all, I was still depressed.

A fter three days, I headed to the south side of Dublin to spend some time with my family. It was perfect timing that one of my cousins was graduating from college two days after I arrived, as I was already desperate for a reprieve from the volunteer program. Her branch of the family was coming up to Dublin from southern Ireland for the graduation, and we were all going out to dinner after, along with my grandmother Frances.

Frances was a petite Irish lady, getting up in years, and battling Alzheimer's. I was a homesick, jet-lagged nervous wreck. We were quite the pair, and neither of us were prepared to eat a whole lot. We both ordered fish and chips and, in hindsight, really should have just split a single order. I think I ate two bites of fish and four chips; Frances did about the same level of damage to her plate. The poor waitress panicked and thought something was wrong with the food when she saw how untouched our plates were. My aunt tried to explain that the fish was delightful; Frances and I were just a pair of unstable folks with no appetite. To her credit, my aunt phrased it a hell of a lot better than that.

The plan was that I'd spend the night at Frances' house, Gaybrook, and head back to my flat the next day. To say that night didn't go well would be like calling Usain Bolt "kind of fast." Understatement of the century. I was mentally and emotionally drained, and despite being so tired I could barely keep my eyes open, I didn't sleep that night. I hadn't slept in days. It would be tough for anyone to get rest on Sheriff's Street, with the constant sirens and yelling and Lord-knows-what-else; piling on some jet lag, homesickness, and mental illness sealed my sleepless fate. By the time I crawled into bed at Gaybrook, I was approaching ninety-six hours without any real sleep. I prayed that sleeping in a house I knew and loved, in a comfortable bed, would let me finally get the rest I so desperately needed. It didn't happen. That night ended up being the second worst night of my life.

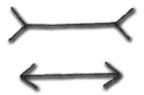

Perspectives

I realize this entire book could use a trigger warning, but this chapter in particular gets its own. Skip to the next chapter if suicidal thoughts/ ideation is too much for you to handle safely.

To be completely honest, I don't entirely remember that night at Gaybrook. I remember tossing and turning for an eternity and getting up to go to the bathroom. I remember digging through the medicine cabinet, climbing back into bed, and Googling what the various pills were and how many I would have to take in order to not wake up the next morning. I remember communicating with Brianna at some point; she was on her way to a concert. I remember the feeling of being swallowed by pain and darkness, and the desperation to do absolutely anything to make it stop. I remember feeling consumed with indescribable sadness, like every broken heart and every pain for every person on the planet was in my heart. I remember the physical pain, as every muscle in my body ached, my head throbbed, and my heart felt like a fiery arrow had been shot right through it. I remember feeling like I was being tortured and knowing that I deserved it. I had made such a mess of my life and had brought so much pain to everyone I loved that I was being punished for it. I remember not answering the phone when someone called, though I don't remember if it was Mom or Brianna, because I couldn't bring myself to keep hurting them.

I remember eventually answering the phone and talking to Mom, still sobbing, heart still pounding, hands still shaking, thoughts still spiraling out of control. Mom had gotten pretty good at talking me down from anxiety attacks, but it had always been in person, not over the phone while we're multiple time zones and half a world away from each other. Her first strategy was simple: count to ten slowly and take a long breath between each number. She'd say one; I'd have trouble breathing or speaking. She'd repeat it until I choked it out in response. Then two. Then three. If we reached ten and I still wasn't regaining control, which didn't often happen, we'd start again back at one.

That night? I could have counted to a million and it wouldn't have changed a thing. I was so far gone that I didn't know if I could ever get back. Luckily, although Mom was halfway around the world from me, she knew the room I was sleeping in; it was her childhood home. She knew I could look out the window and see the streetlights and house across the street. She knew I could hear the peace of Mount Merrion. And she knew there was a bookshelf above my bed. She told me to grab a book, any book, from the shelf. There was only one I recognized: Horrible Harry. Growing up, it was one of my favorite books.

If you aren't familiar with Horrible Harry, it's a series of books with pretty much the same premise in every single one:

there's a kid named Harry, and he's an absolute pest. He doesn't do anything hugely damaging since he's in, like, second grade, but the little twerp is just a general nuisance to society. In every book, Harry does something to screw up whatever is going on, his friends help him out, and we reach a very predictable ending where Harry learns from his mistakes/promises not to do it again/makes amends for whatever he did. In the third grade, I couldn't get enough of Horrible Harry. Now? Not so much. I haven't touched a Horrible Harry book since Ireland. But anyway, Mom told me to grab a book, and I went with my man Harry. She needed me to focus on something else—anything else—to get through the night, so she had me read Horrible Harry out loud to her. I couldn't tell you if I read a page, a chapter, or the entire thing cover-to-cover, but after enough time, the exhaustion finally took hold and mercifully granted me a precious few hours of sleep.

I don't remember much about the following day, but I have to believe it was a hellacious time. As I mentioned, I was staying with Frances, my kind, compassionate, soulful grandmother battling Alzheimer's. She was at the point where she had a vague understanding of what was going on in the world, but everything in her brain was quite muddled. It was almost impossible to have a conversation with her, so she had no concrete awareness of what I was going through—which is also why I didn't disturb her the night before to ask for help. She passed away a few years back, but what I'll never forget about Frances is that despite not knowing the extent of my pain or its cause, in her heart she understood that I was struggling.

By the time I got up, she had already been to the shops up the street and bought my favorite apple tart and the largest bag of

KitKats I've seen outside America. That bag put Costco to shame. I have no idea where she got them. Might have robbed a KitKat factory for all I know. To be clear, I'm not that into KitKats. There's nothing wrong with them, they're a perfectly acceptable candy, but I couldn't possibly have a more neutral stance on them. But Frances—muddled brain and all—seemed to have decided that KitKats were the best move she could make for me. Every time I entered the kitchen, she'd give me KitKats. I found KitKats on the shelf next to my bed. When she was sitting in her chair by a sunny window and I walked by, she'd hand me more KitKats. I found a couple of them in the bathroom. And, of course, there was the massive bag always in the kitchen ready for the taking. To this day, I don't exactly know what her game plan was with the KitKats; but, to her credit, while the KitKats may not have cured my depression, they certainly didn't make it any worse.

While writing this chapter, I asked Brianna if she could send me anything she recalled from that night, to fill in the gaps in my timeline. After reading what she wrote, though, I realized I had stumbled across something incredibly important that I could never have captured on my own: perspective.

I can't know what it feels like to try to support me in my darkest days. I will never experience a perspective other than my own, and my perspective is limited. (I also don't know if a mentally ill person is the most reliable narrator, but that's beside the point). I'm writing it all exactly as I remember it, but that's precisely the problem: it's how *I* remembered it. If the Wizard of Oz and Wicked musicals taught us anything, it's that perspective is everything. Brianna has her story of that night. Mom has her story of that night. Brianna's friends have their stories from that night. All of those stories piece together to create a more thorough picture of what a person experiencing a mental crisis looks like, and how it can appear to those who love them.

Edited only to change names and get verb tense/pronouns sorted out, here are some of their memories of that night.

Brianna

We were on our way to a Kid Cudi concert, which in many ways ended up more appropriate than expected. It was me and two friends, Savini and Nabeel, and I was driving Mom's old Pontiac. I was driving when you started texting, and I know I shouldn't text and drive, but they were popping up above the directions on the GPS screen and I couldn't not see them.

I don't remember exactly which message it was that made me realize that something was very wrong, but I think it was something along the lines of "I don't want to be here anymore." You were in Ireland, so far away, both geographically and mentally, and for some reason all I kept thinking of were knives. I don't know why, it's not like you'd ever been a cutter, but the only image in my head was you walking toward a knife block in the kitchen alone at night.

I was trying to multitask and respond with one hand and keep us on the highway with the other, but at a certain point, I pulled off onto the shoulder and just started hyperventilating and sobbing. You were telling me that you were ready to end it and that it wasn't worth it. I was trying to call you and you weren't answering. Savini and Nabeel had no idea what was happening and were trying to console me, but I was incoherent, trying to call you and text you without getting any response.

I was so sure that I was never going to see you again, and I felt like my body was melting. It was the most out-of-body experience ever. I felt like I was floating above my sobbing self on the side of a San Diego freeway. At that moment, everything that felt important suddenly felt jarringly stupid and life felt absurdly fragile, and I felt like my sadness was so huge that it was going to crush me.

I called Mom and Dad to try to do something, anything, but I was so incoherent when they first picked up the phone that they didn't know who it was. I think they actually might have hung up on me (classic Nelson family communication lapse), because I remember Savini having to call from her phone, too. Once I started talking to Mom and was struck by the dissonance of her non-shock, a wave of realization washed over me. I had been shielded, but this wasn't the first time. This wasn't new.

My phone was also nearly dead, so Savini took the wheel and drove us to a Burger King to charge it. I just remember sitting on the floor next to a smushed fry, charging my phone under a laminate table. A child eating his chicken nuggets stared at me as I continued to cry quietly into the phone. I remember that Dad's friend happened to be over for dinner that night because once everyone was calm enough to speak, he made a comment about how much I clearly loved you. I remember thinking that was a stupid comment, because what kind of psycho wouldn't be devastated by her sister trying to kill herself?

Once I was starting to understand more, Mom said that my freaking out had scared you a lot, too, which made me so angry[10]. So angry that this was all being kept from me, and so incredibly angry at what I perceived to be relative indifference from Mom and Dad. I wanted to shake them. I wanted to scream at them and ask how the fuck they would feel if we had lost you. I was blindsided by everyone else not being blindsided.

---

[10] I mostly wanted this to be an unfiltered perspective, but I have to set the record straight on this one real quick. Brianna's reaction hadn't scared me at all. I was petrified from the thoughts screaming inside my head; nothing and no one could have made things any worse.

Savini and Nabeel told me we could go home and that we didn't need to go to the concert. But I knew that wouldn't help anything, and I wasn't ready to just sit at home with my thoughts. I think it was the first time I was really scared to be inside my head. I just kept trying to understand what was happening in your head, and I couldn't [11]. We still went, and it was a great concert, but I went to the bathroom twice to throw up because I just kept thinking about you and knives, and it made me physically ill.

It is funny to me that the whole night has so many details that are so clear in my memory, but the weeks or so after are a complete fog. I have no idea what our first conversation after was like, I don't remember talking to Mom about it right after—just nothing. It was like the night was a wound, and I was able to form scar tissue for everything else after that. I just couldn't quite form it quickly enough for that night.

I don't really know how to end this. I guess there isn't an end, and maybe that's the point. But it was definitely a start. A beginning of being jarred into a completely different reality, with a completely different level of empathy for mental health challenges than I had ever before appreciated, and a completely different level of comprehension of what the average person could be going through at any given moment.

So, I suppose it was the end of my naïveté in a lot of ways, and the start of trying to understand.

Mom

Friday 1 p.m. PST/ 9 p.m. Ireland:
I called you while you were in Gaybrook, just to say hello, after your dinner out with the family. We talked for a while—mostly you were

---

[11] Join the club. Nobody knew what was going on up there…myself included.

feeling unsure about being there, and I was encouraging you to take it one day at a time.

Friday 4 p.m. PST/ midnight Ireland:
You texted me to ask me if you could give Brianna a call, as you were having trouble sleeping. I said sure.

Friday 7:30 p.m. PST/ 3:30 a.m. Ireland:
Savini called. I don't really remember what the gist of it was, except that Brianna was super worried about you and was afraid that you were suicidal. I told Savini to tell Brianna to hang up the phone, and I would call you right away. I called you, and I think I also asked Dad to call Brianna back and let her know that I was talking to you.

Friday 8 p.m. PST/ 4 a.m. Ireland:
I talked to you, trying to get you to calm down and just try to go to sleep. You mentioned that the kitchen knives were downstairs, but I didn't really think you would actually hurt yourself if I could get you to calm down sufficiently to sleep. I had you count down from 100 a few times and take deep breaths until you were slightly more coherent. We talked for quite a while about nothing in particular, and then I suggested that you read a book, as a way to just occupy your mind until you fell asleep. You picked one of the Horrible Harry books, and I had you start reading it aloud to me. Eventually, I got you to settle down and read. I suggested that if you were still awake in an hour, you could call me back. I didn't hear back from you that evening, so I assumed you had actually finally fallen asleep. I then talked to Dad and his friend for a while. None of us were sure what to do, other than support you and hope that you would

settle down soon. We did think it was the right experience for you, but we were unsure how to support you until you settled in.

My general memory of that week was a combination of 50% sleep deprivation and 50% anxiety that prevented you from thinking clearly. Once you were able to start sleeping, you were still very anxious, but we were at least able to have a rational conversation. One thing that did surprise me was that the night after you flew back home, you had a panic attack.

Throughout the entire experience of reliving my darkest moments while writing this book, this section right here is the only one that truly put my stomach in knots. This is the only section I'm scared about. I am afraid I lack the delicacy needed to perfectly articulate what I'm trying to say without hurting Mom. But this book is about the truth, and it seems just as important to share the conflicts and contradictions as it is to share the times that we were all on the same page.

For context, my immediate family has never been great at communicating, especially when things get tough. We often joke about how bad our communication is: when Dad doesn't know we had dinner plans; when Mom doesn't know Brianna is leaving the state; when Grandma doesn't know I'm getting an apartment; or any other disconnect. It can be mildly entertaining when it's on that level, but it has also proven to be one of the worst termites in our family's roots over the years. When things are hard, we are a sweep-it-under-the-rug kind of family.

Whenever Brianna and I got in arguments as kids, we were sent to our rooms to cool off, and that was it. No follow-up, no significant discussion. Cool off and move on. We got into a little tiff at Grandma's house when we couldn't have been much older than early elementary school and were floored when she expected us to talk it out after we had calmed down. It wasn't how we normally operated, and to this day still isn't how we operate as a family. Brianna and I have come a long way in recent years to lean on each other more, but it hasn't been easy, and it certainly doesn't come naturally.

Asking my family to write their perspectives on that night in Ireland was eye-opening. When I read Brianna's experience, I was struck with three main thoughts: she really does understand me like nobody else, what she described as going on in her head was very similar to what goes on in mine when I'm in a depressive episode, and I probably owe her Kid Cudi tickets. I didn't get particularly emotional reading what she wrote; I just felt like I needed to give her a big ol' hug and an even bigger "thank you," (She's a hugger, but I'm not, so my offering a hug is a *huge* deal). She doesn't remember exactly what I said. I don't remember exactly what I said. But I was halfway around the world, hurtling towards suicide, and she knew it without a shadow of a doubt.

On the other hand, when I read Mom's experience, I cried —hard. Mom is a brilliant, analytical woman. She solves problems one step at a time, and there is no situation she can't come up with a plan to conquer. She is fantastic in a crisis, largely because of her ability to keep a level head. Reading her experience, I realized that my inability to communicate what I was really going through meant that her step-by-step process never had a chance of working out. It was like she had prepared a beautiful strategy and game plan for a basketball game, but I was playing soccer. It was an ideal step-by-step process for a sleep-deprived, jet-lagged, homesick person experiencing a little bit of anxiety and culture shock, but it was not the right process for a sleep-deprived, jet-lagged, depressed, and suicidal person.

In her defense, I never told her I was suicidal or having any sort of suicidal ideations. Not that night, nor any other time the thoughts had been bouncing around my head. I thought I had alluded to it sufficiently. I thought I had danced around it to the point that I didn't actually have to say it and that it was clearly understood. I thought saying things like "I want to be done" or "I can't do this anymore" were enough to let Mom put two and two together. Evidently, such was not the case. In hindsight, it comes as no surprise that she didn't think I would actually hurt myself. I understand why she would try to see the positive in my elusive statements, and not jump to the conclusion that I was a danger to myself. It's the last conclusion any parent would want to jump to, so it makes perfect sense that her instinct wouldn't allow her to assume I was suicidal. As a family, we were all wildly out of our depth. None of us had experienced mental illness before, knew what to expect, knew the extent to which it could escalate, or knew how to be fully supportive.

Many of the things I chose not to share with family, friends, or the rest of the world were due to a certain level of shame. I was embarrassed by the lack of control over my own life. But when it came to *ending* my life, I wasn't ashamed by it, or anything even remotely close that. I didn't talk about it because I was terrified of it. In my mind, not outwardly admitting it was my feeble attempt at not allowing those thoughts to hold power over my family and me. But at the same time, I knew I needed help.

I should have said it. Whether by text, email, carrier pigeon, smoke signals, morse code, or pony express, I should have said it clear as day. *I want to die. I do not want to be alive anymore. I want to take my own life. I am having suicidal thoughts.* But I didn't. My fear consumed me, and I was determined not to validate those thoughts and feelings. I was so caught up in taking power away from my suicidal thoughts that I didn't see I was also taking away opportunities for my loved ones to support me.

Brianna, who has been my protector from the day I arrived on planet Earth[12], was able to read between my sobbing, blurry lines and see that I was moments away from killing myself—but she had no plan to help me. Our trademark Nelson-family lack of communication had built barriers that shut her out of my attempted recovery. My lack of communication had built a barrier that shut Mom out from truly seeing the depth of my pain. That night was the imperfect storm that shone a light on both of those shortcomings. Individually, neither of them had the whole picture. Brianna had the pallet, and Mom had the canvas. But because each of them had only half a sense of what I was going through, neither of them could fully understand what was happening.

There aren't many things I regret in my life. I wish I'd stuck with soccer instead of basketball when I was in high school. I wish I'd appreciated my lightning-fast metabolism as a highly active teenager. I wish I'd stuck with learning Spanish and the guitar. After reading Mom's perspective, I have a new biggest regret in life: I wish I'd been completely transparent with what I was going through, and much clearer with what I needed. Brianna

---

[12] In one of the very first photos that we have of Brianna and I, she's in the hospital bed with Mom the day I was born, counting to verify that I did, in fact, have all ten fingers.

could understand that I was suffering, but didn't know what I needed. Mom knew what I needed, based on what she *thought* I was going through. My inability, or lack of willingness, to fully communicate with my family—whether caused by fear, shame, childhood habits, or something else entirely—was nearly deadly.

I'm not saying that a sit-down meeting with the whole family and getting everyone on the same page is the cure for depression. But in a crisis, when lives are hanging in the balance, allowing someone to have the complete picture is essential. I took that opportunity away from my support system by sharing different sides of myself with each of them. In truth, this book is probably the first time that all of them will get the unfiltered reality of everything I was feeling, thinking, and fearing at that time.

Mrs. Fix-It

The morning after the crisis, Mom called my Aunt Bernie to ask for help. Mark (one of Mom's brothers) and his wife, Bernie, lived next door to Frances. They have three daughters who are close in age to Brianna and me, and we've always had a great relationship with them. Mom knew Frances wasn't in a state to take care of me, and there probably weren't enough KitKats in the world to sustain her pace, but Bernie had been helping out taking care of Frances for a few years.

If you were paying attention to the start of the book—particularly the dedication—the name "Bernie" might ring a bell. Needless to say, Bernie said yes in a heartbeat. She would take me in. When I got home from work that night, I was directed to collect my things from Frances' house, take a few KitKats for the long walk through the hole in the hedge, and report to Mark and Bernie's home next door. The family had already eaten dinner, but she had a warm plate of leftovers ready and waiting for me.

The thing I will never forget, and forever be grateful for, was how calm and collected Bernie was about everything. She had the perfect balance of showing unconditional love for me and compassion for my situation but spending no time pitying or babying me. We weren't going to have deep emotional conversations to unpack my tragic story, we weren't going to delicately suggest things that might be helpful, and we weren't going to dwell on how horrific the previous night had been or how catastrophic it could have become. There were jobs to do to get things sorted out, and we were going to get them done. Bernie was putting me back together one piece at a time, and I will always cherish that she never once made me feel broken.

Our first order of business was figuring out how to get me to sleep. I am a firm believer that few issues in life can't be improved with a glass of water and a good night's sleep. Bernie marched me up to the local chemist, explained the problem, and within twenty minutes we were out the door with some sort of sleeping draught. I was told to take five milliliters at bedtime. I had my doubts that a measly five milliliters were going to be enough to knock me out; I was wrong. Very, very wrong.

For starters, the stuff smelled heinous. The indescribable stench haunts me to this day. Bernie never had to check in that I had taken it each evening because the stink was unavoidable. The whole house knew whether I'd opened the bottle, and it wouldn't surprise me if neighbors down the block could also smell it. After choking down the rancid syrup, I had maybe ten minutes before I'd be dead to the world. It was like NyQuil on steroids. I was out colder than a concussed football player in Antarctica. The first night I took it, I flopped down on the couch and didn't move for fourteen hours. The next night was another twelve hours. I'm sure the starting level of sleep deprivation was a contributing factor, but man…that nasty sleeping potion was a game-changer.

Task number two was retrieving my stuff from the terrible flat. Luckily, I hadn't unpacked much since there wasn't any space to do so. One thing to know about Bernie (if you hadn't already picked up on it) is that she is one tough cookie. She is a strong, fearless woman, and I've never seen her scared—or even thrown off—by anything. That is, except for my metal grate front door. When I whipped out the first key to crank that bad boy up, I realized by her reaction alone that this place was, in fact, pretty awful. Her face showed a combination of shock and sheer disgust. I knew I was in a different country with a different culture, and although I'd been to Ireland many times before, we'd always stayed with family. I had feared that I'd exaggerated the state of my flat, simply because it was something so different, but Bernie's reaction validated everything I had thought. It was downright horrible. We must have been in and out of there in ten minutes flat; if we were cartoon characters, there would have been a Bernie-and-Sinéad-sized hole blasted right through that damn grate.

When we got back home, Bernie told my Uncle Mark about the grate. When her daughters got home from work, she told them about the grate. When my Great-Uncle Billy and his wife, Anne, came over for dinner that night, Bernie told them about the grate as well. Uncle Billy was another tough-as-nails Irishman, with a handshake grip that could break your fingers and well-worn hands from years of working on cars. He jokingly asked where my flat was, surprised that I was staying anywhere in Dublin that would require said metal grate. I told him my address, and I'm reasonably confident he thought I was either pulling his leg or totally mixed up with my directions. When I started describing the general area and cross streets, he realized that I was, in fact, telling the truth. He was floored at where they'd placed me. I must confess, seeing Bernie and Uncle Billy's reactions to my housing situation certainly validated how freaked out I had been by the whole debacle.

The last, but most significant, thing Bernie helped take care of was getting me the hell out of Ireland. Don't get me wrong; I love Ireland. I will always love Ireland. I believe it is undoubtedly the greatest country in the world. But at that time, I needed to get out of there before I was really in too deep. Mom had plans to stop in Ireland for a few days on her way to India for a business trip about a week after I arrived, which proved to be perfect timing.

Once Mom got settled in, she headed in to chat with Bernie as I went off to another day of work. So far, Mom's only perspective on the whole situation had been mine; while I thought I was being a perfectly reliable narrator, it made sense that she would want a little corroboration. Perhaps aggressively reminding Mom on the phone before she arrived that I didn't need her permission to leave—and that I knew where the airport bus stop was and could change a flight reservation on my own—didn't give me the most credibility.

Just as she had with me, Bernie sat down with Mom and, with no fussing or messing about, explained that what I was looking for was not going to happen in Ireland. The landscape of youth sports in the United States compared to youth sports in Ireland are apples and oranges. The culture is completely different, and the way I wanted to use sports as a vessel of change just wasn't in the cards in Ireland. Mental and emotional stability aside, the volunteer program was never going to be what I was looking for. Even if I wasn't in a depressive episode, the year would have been a constant struggle between what I believed in and what I was expected to do.

In a whirlwind of nine days, I had arrived in Ireland, fallen apart in Ireland, and come to the realization that Ireland was not the right move for me. Once again, I didn't know the right move; I just knew this had been yet another wrong move. I also knew that I was out of ideas on what my next move could possibly be.

Running Out of Options

Here's the issue with running from your problems: you can only run so far until you have to start actually working towards something. Kind of like how if you drive North forever, literally around the world, you will ultimately end up going South. The University of Oregon wasn't right. Community college wasn't right. University College Cork wasn't right. Volunteering in Ireland wasn't right. I had run from every place I'd been and ended up right back where I'd started: at home, depressed, and wondering what the hell I was supposed to do next.

There's a book I used to read as a kid called *Fortunately*[13]. I don't entirely remember the plot, but each sentence bounces back and forth between "fortunately" and "unfortunately." For example:

Fortunately, Ned was invited to a surprise party.

---

[13] Charlip, Remy. *Fortunately* First Aladdin Books edition, Aladdin Books; Maxwell Macmillan Canada; Maxwell Macmillan International, 1993.

Unfortunately, the party was a thousand miles away.

Fortunately, a friend loaned Ned an airplane.

Unfortunately, the motor exploded.

You get the gist. By the time I left Ireland, I was starting to feel a lot like Ned (minus the exploded airplane). Fortunately, I had found a great volunteer program. Unfortunately, it was a bit of a sham. Fortunately, it crumbled quickly enough that I had time to go back to college without missing any time. Unfortunately, it was too late to apply to any schools. Fortunately, I could re-enroll at Oregon because it had been less than a year since I dropped out. Unfortunately, I was terrified to go back. Fortunately, Mom convinced me to give it another try. Unfortunately, it was too late to find anywhere to live. Fortunately, I could apply to live in the freshman dorms again, even though I was a sophomore. Unfortunately, I applied so late that all the dorms were full. Fortunately, they had "expanded housing," where students could live temporarily until a dorm opened up. Unfortunately, this "expanded housing" was awfully reminiscent of military barracks I'd seen in movies. Fortunately, I got along well with the other girls living in expanded housings. Unfortunately, we all got split into different dorms as rooms opened up.

And the ultimate "unfortunately" of them all…I was still very depressed. I developed the roots of an incredibly toxic relationship with my depression, where I hated it and hated myself for how I felt. I was angry at my demented brain, and that anger only made the bad days pile up even faster. Each time I had a bad day, Mom hoped there was some external reason for it: not yet settled in because of the moves, overwhelmed with my class schedule, nervous about making new friends, the works.

But the bottom line was that I was terrified—absolutely terrified. Oregon brought back horrible memories of the darkest times of my life, and I was petrified to end up back in that darkness. When I arrived, things somehow managed to get even worse. What I thought was rock bottom, wasn't. What I thought were my darkest days, weren't. I was spiraling not into darkness, but absolute emptiness. I could feel myself losing my grip every single day. Once again, my gut was screaming at me that this was wrong. I had to run. I had started to understand that running away from my problems wasn't going to fix things, so I started researching residential depression treatment programs. Maybe if I ran towards help, rather than away from pain, things could improve.

Mom and I Skyped each other regularly (#tbt to the ancient pre-FaceTime days), but I was never able to express to her how awful I was feeling. I couldn't find the words, didn't think the timing was right, or just plain didn't want to tell her. Whatever the reason, I couldn't bring myself to look her in the eye and tell her what I was feeling. While researching my own history for this book, I came across the email where I finally found the words:

> Hi Mom,
> Do you think you might have time to Skype tonight? I know we didn't want to get stuck in the routine of calling every night, but I feel like I lost all the hope I had yesterday morning. It just seems like everything I find that helps me get through a couple more hours just does that - get me through a couple hours. Then I'm back to where I was, but without the new "hope-inducer".

I'm trying to just hang on until the appointment on Monday - (I had scheduled an appointment with a therapist at the campus health center) - *but then I remember that after Monday I have to hang on until Tuesday, then Wednesday, then Thursday, and on and on and on. And that's when I stop wanting to do it anymore.*

Whenever I try to say it on the phone I just start crying and freaking out, so I'm writing this part. Mom, I'm terrified. I don't know what's happening to me, I don't know why, and I can't ever see it being completely better. I know that the hopeless part is because of the disease, but I've never had anything make me feel so helpless. It's ruining my life, and I just want it to be over. I hate myself. I hate that I'm weak, and vulnerable. I hate that I don't even know how to fake it anymore. It feels like I have completely lost Sinéad. I have a Taylor Swift quote for everything, and the one that keeps running through my head is "I'd like to be my old self again, but I'm still trying to find her". The outside is still the same, but I feel completely empty inside - just a shell of myself. On bad days I feel devastated, on good days I don't feel anything at all. I'm really scared that I'll never be regular Sinéad again, let alone happy Sinéad.

I want to be able to focus on just getting better, and not try to be dealing with school while doing so. I know what being homesick feels like, I know what my adjustment issues feel like, and I know what the minor depression I've been dealing with for months feels like. But this is different. I don't know when it started, but this depression is much, much worse. Even at home, my regular "happy things" didn't matter as much. Even when I was eating

74

ice cream, or hanging out with Kevin, or watching tv with dad,
it just didn't matter. I was still unhappy.

Last time at Oregon, I just wanted to leave. I didn't care where I
went, I just wanted to not be at Oregon. I didn't see a point to
being a student. This time is the opposite. I know that I need to
be a student, so I can become a teacher. But I need to get better
before I can really do that. I don't know if that means leaving
Oregon to find a program that will really get me better, and then
coming back. But I really do believe that I need to focus on
getting better before I can focus on the future.

Mom, ever the level-headed realist, didn't let me run. I don't
know if she was starting to figure out that there wasn't a place on
earth that could "fix" me, or if she was just punting the problem.
Either way, I was staying put in Eugene, Oregon.

About a mile off-campus, you'll find Autzen Stadium,
Oregon's massive, legendary, stunning football stadium. The walk
from campus to Autzen is equally legendary— over the
Willamette river and through the woods of Alton Baker Park. In
late October, when I was still ages from the freedom of winter
break, I decided to take a walk out towards Autzen. It was
pouring rain, and there wasn't a football game or any other event.
I just needed to walk. Before I left for my walk, I wrote some
letters: one to Mom and Dad, one to Brianna, one to Grandma, one
to a mentor, and one to my friends. It might have been overkill to
write so many letters, but I didn't want there to be any confusion
or conflicting stories that I couldn't later explain. I left the letters
on my pillow, where they'd be easily found once anyone realized I
was gone.

It was pouring rain as I headed to the river; or, more specifically, as I headed to the bridge. The river gets deeper and moves swiftly when it's raining, but it doesn't get deep enough to submerge the rocks below. Along the bridge, there are a few benches so that you can admire the view of the Willamette River. I was the only one out there, probably because it was a late October evening and rain was relentlessly bucketing down. As I walked, I wondered how I would feel when I reached the bridge. Scared? Sad? Guilty? Happy?

I felt none of those. I felt peace, combined with a heavy relief. It felt like finishing a test you pulled an all-nighter studying for but walking out knowing that you failed. It's battling through multiple overtime periods in a game only to lose at the final buzzer. It's setting down a weight you've carried for miles, only to realize you're nowhere close to your destination. Too exhausted to feel any sort of excitement, but a sense of calm that comes with knowing the battle is done. It certainly hasn't been won, but at least it's over.

I got to the bridge and sat down on the bench, letting the rain wash over me. Raindrops had drenched my beanie on the way over, so the droplets scurried down my skin. I was already soaked to the skin from the walk, every inch of me drenched. My sister makes fun of me for being so white that I turn blue in the cold; she's not wrong. My palms started to turn blue as I sat on the bench. I sat. And sat. And sat. And continued to sit. I hadn't brought my phone or anything with me (what would be the use?), so I don't actually know how long I sat there. It might have been ten minutes. It might have been four hours.

All I do know is that sitting there—freezing my ass off, probably catching pneumonia, and hands getting irreparably pruney—for a fleeting moment, I felt okay. I didn't feel cold. I didn't feel wet. I didn't feel the wind. Mercifully, I didn't feel sad. I certainly didn't feel anything on the spectrum of "happy," but I felt solidly okay. It wasn't even the blah feeling I had come to cherish. It was genuinely, wholeheartedly, beautifully okay. I felt like I had taken a full breath for the first time in months. It was just one moment, one breath, but it was something. Kind of like when there's a TV character in a coma and their eyes flutter, if only for a split second. Or when you're trying to power a lightbulb from a lemon, and you get a teeny burst of light. It's barely a flicker, but it's something.

About a year later, Taylor Swift released an impeccable album, *1989*, with one of my all-time favorite lyrics. It's on a song called Clean, which is also an incredibly therapeutic track with the lyric: "Rain came pouring down when I was drowning, that's when I could finally breathe."
If I had to choose a single lyric to capture every fiber of my being at that time, that masterpiece right there would be the one. I swear she looked into my soul and pulled out the most poetic words to describe that moment in the pouring rain on the bridge. Truth be told, I don't know what it is about the rain that I find so comforting. While others may find it dreary and depressing, I find it soothing. Any day with rain in the forecast is a day I'm looking forward to.

As human beings, you never know what the next day will hold. You never actually know if you'll be happy or sad, hot or cold, or anything else. You can guess based on previous days…if it's July and you'll be spending the next day at Disneyland, you can bank on happy and hot. Going to a funeral in Ireland? Pretty safe to assume cold and sad. In a depressive episode, all you can count on is some variant of sad. It could be an angry sad, a frustrated sad, a grieving sad, an exhausted sad, or just plain, old-fashioned sad. When you have a flicker of not being sad, it becomes everything you hold on to.

I had been losing my grip because, for so long, I'd had no flickers. Times that should have been joyous weren't as delightful as I wanted them to be, and the guilt I piled on myself for not feeling happy buried any chance of a flicker. But for some reason —a reason I will probably never know—that day I got the most crucial flicker of my life. Maybe it was God, maybe it was a deep part of me that had finally fought to the surface, maybe it was fate, maybe it was Maybelline, or maybe it was something else entirely. No matter the source, it was a flicker, and it gave me something to hold onto. It gave me a glimpse of a feeling I thought was long gone. It got me off the bench, off the bridge, and walking back to campus. It got me back to my room to take the letters and tear them to shreds.

I'd love to end the book here and say that the rain saved my life, and everything was happy daisies from there on out; but as anyone who has ever dealt with mental illness can tell you, that's not how it works. The next day was pretty bad again, and the next, and the next, and the next. They were generally bad days straight through another four months. But slowly, one minuscule step at a time, things started to improve. The darkest days were fewer and farther between. The blah days became more frequent. The blah days started evolving to solidly okay days. And somewhere along the way, the good days started to shine through. It **was** like putting food coloring in vanilla icing. It starts with a single drop; the more you stir, the more it spreads. A dot of color becomes a tie-dye style swirl of color, and eventually takes over the entire bowl of icing. The good days began to outnumber the bad. Just as the bumper stickers and t-shirts and mugs and silicone bracelets claimed it would…it got better.

In hindsight, I would not recommend darn near anything about how I approached that depressive episode. I sought very little treatment or support, never fully understood what was going on, and really only worked to make sense of it in the years that followed. It did ultimately get better, but all I can truly give myself credit for is managing to hold on long enough to get through it. My second episode…now that's a whole other story. Or, shall I say, a whole other set of chapters in this book.

Episode Two

August 2018 to Present

Nine for Nine

L et's start by breaking down the basics: what makes someone a crazy? Or, in my particular case, what makes someone a clinically depressed crazy? Major recurrent depression is my main course, but I also got a side of anxiety and a little pinch of PTSD sprinkled on top. One of my therapists suspected I had ADHD, but apparently, my out-of-control thoughts were just some good old-fashioned anxiety. This book is pretty heavily focused on depression since that's my number one wheelhouse, but that is far from the only mental illness people face every day. There are about 150 different disorders in the DSM-V, down from 170-ish in DSM-IV. If I happen to get hit with another whammy, I'll write another book about it; but for my sake, let's pray that I don't end up with enough material for a sequel.

According to the Diagnostic and Statistical Manual of Mental Disorders (DSM-V), there are nine depressive symptoms[14]. To be "officially" depressed, you need to have experienced five or more symptoms in the same two-week period, and (of course) you need to have a "depressed mood." It's kind of like the world's worst ice cream sundae. You have to start with the ice cream base (depressed mood), and then you get to pick at least four other toppings (symptoms) to go with your depressed mood. The only real difference is that an ice cream sundae is delightful, and clinical depression is…not so much.

Number One: Depressed mood
Most of the day, nearly every day; may be subjective (e.g., feels sad, empty, hopeless) or observed by others (e.g., appears tearful); in children and adolescents, can be irritable mood.

I find technical descriptions of mental health symptoms to be highly entertaining. They are absolute comedy. I like to imagine a bunch of highly educated doctors, psychiatrists, neurologists, and the like all sitting around a table staring at a depressed kid, trying to describe their issues in scientific terms.

Doc 1: We have to get this language figured out, but this example kid just *won't. stop. crying.*

Doc 2: I don't know if "won't stop crying" is official enough. Can we spice it up a bit? Throw some SAT words at it and see if they stick?

Doc 3: Hmmm, good call, Doc 2. Let's make this very subjective moment as objective as possible.

---

[14] CBS Publishers & Distributors, Pvt. Ltd. (2017). Diagnostic and Statistical Manual of Mental Disorders: DSM-5.

Doc 1: What if we say they have to be visibly upset?

Doc 2: Too vague. I was visibly upset last week when I lost my good stethoscope! *laughs in Doctor*

Doc 1: Could we just say that they are crying?

Doc 2: I don't think that'll work either. Even when this human faucet isn't actively crying, it still looks like we're no more than two words away from the floodgates opening.

Doc 3: How about "looks sad"?

Doc 2: Not doctor-y enough.

Doc 1: How about they "appear tearful"?

Doc 2: NAILED IT. Write that down.

Incidentally, I don't think I appeared particularly tearful to people outside of my family. I've always been a pretty rotten liar, but somehow when it came to convincing people that I was totally fine, I was a master. Granted, there were a few days that I needed to just hide from the world so as not to "appear tearful" to strangers, coworkers, bosses, and the general public. But for the most part, I think I masked my tearfulness pretty well. Actually, I know I masked it well because when I finally told people what was going on, it was totally out of left field for them.

A quality excuse and a good fake laugh are pretty much all you need to avoid appearing tearful. If I were entering a talent show, fake laughing would be my act, and I would win that show by a landslide. I'm gonna go out on a limb and say that my fake laughter could put some Oscar winners to shame. Meryl Streep ain't got nothing on my "time to look happy so nobody knows I am dying inside!" laughter. I can even tailor the fake laugh to fit each individual situation perfectly.

If you just need a small chuckle, you can plop on a fake smile and just kind of push air out of your nose in short bursts. If it's something that's supposed to be knee-slapping hilarious, pull your eyebrows up as far as you possibly can and push air from your smiling mouth. And if needed, you can always just go all the way to silent laughter.

From my experience, the most effective excuses are the ones you can reuse time and time again. My personal go-to is "My neighbors were so loud last night I could barely sleep!" It's a more strategic excuse than you might think. Using it once puts it in place for future necessity; these mythical neighbors of yours could be very loud multiple times a week. Nobody will call your bluff, and you don't really need to prove it. If you play it right, people will start assuming the noisy neighbors as the root of any of your cranky exhaustion. It's the excuse that keeps on excusing.

Part two of depressed mood is the trifecta. The three little pigs. The Lion, the Witch, and the Wardrobe. The Big Three[15]. The Deathly Hallows: Sadness, emptiness, and hopelessness. Sadness is pretty obvious. Most people think of sadness when it comes to depression, which is why misinformed, or under-informed people like to offer some variant of "have you tried being happy?" as their first remedial suggestion.

I had a teacher once who said that if you start a statement about someone with "Bless his/her heart…" then you can say anything you want and it's fine. So, for those of you who suggest to depressed folks that they should just try being happy and choosing positivity every morning: Bless your heart, but you are

---

[15] In this house we acknowledge Steph/Klay/Draymond and only Steph/Klay/Draymond as the Big Three. Get out of here with your LeBron/Wade/Bosh or Pierce/Garnett/Allen trios.

an absolute doofus. I would love to choose happiness. I would love to be not depressed. That would be undeniably preferable. But if I could make that choice, don't you think I would have by now? Why would anybody wake up in the morning and choose to be sad? You'd never tell a person with cancer to try not having cancer, and you wouldn't suggest that a person with paraplegia try to have fully functioning legs. So why are you telling a depressed person to try not to be depressed? DON'T YOU THINK I WOULD HAVE DONE THAT BY NOW IF IT WAS AN OPTION? Sorry for yelling. I got carried away. The point is, sadness sucks and I can't imagine a single person on planet earth who would choose to be sad 24/7.

Next up is emptiness. Invisibility. Absolutely nothing at all. It may sound weird, but in the darkest depths of a depressive episode, emptiness was one of my favorite symptoms. The days when I felt nothing at all were the best days. We called them my "blah" days because that was the extent of what I felt. Blah. Completely numb. Unremarkable. Entirely vacant. I was lucky that my depression didn't manifest itself in substance abuse, but on those blah days, it makes complete sense why so many people struggling with mental illness do turn to substances. If your options are feeling never-ending pain and sadness, or feeling nothing at all, it's hard not to lean towards feeling absolutely nothing.

When I started taking lithium to help stabilize my mood, my biggest hesitation against taking it was that the stabilization would turn into something along the lines of emptiness, but that was a risk I was gladly willing to take. Once again, I evaluated the two options. Option 1 was a roller coaster of really sad and really happy days. On a scale of 1–10, with 1 being suicidal thoughts and

10 being the greatest day in human existence, I'd have more 9s and 10s, but also more 1s and 2s. Option 2 was a relative plateau of not-that-sad and moderately happy. Lots of 4 through 7s, and not much at either end of the scale. From that point of view, it was a pretty easy choice. Forego the highest highs to prevent the lowest lows.

Then there's hopelessness. Hopelessness is an asshole, plain and simple. Imagine breaking both of your legs and having to relearn how to walk. You do the rehab, go to physical therapy, and learn all over again, knowing there's a solid 50/50 chance you're going to snap your femurs again. You've been walking and running for a while—maybe just a few months, maybe decades—and you break your legs again. Back to the wheelchair. Back to square one. You have to learn how to walk for a third time. As an added bonus this time around, there's now an 80% chance you'll break your legs and have to relearn again. After recovering the third time, you're all but guaranteed to break them a fourth time. Then a fifth. And a sixth. Sticking with the devil you know, accepting your wheelchair-bound fate, starts to sound more and more appealing with each set of broken legs.

Someone with hope might be able to focus on the 50% chance of not having a second episode. Or the 20% chance of not having a third episode. Or the 5% chance of not having a fourth episode. But in the middle of a depressive episode, you don't have the luxury of hope. All you see is an exponential growth graph normally used for charting rabbit reproduction, but now it's charting your likelihood of more misery.

I read a quote on Tumblr: "Mental illness is like fighting a war where the enemy's strategy is to convince you that the war isn't actually happening." And honestly, how messed up is that?

How do you expect me to win a fight that you are determined to tell me doesn't even exist? You're a real punk for that, hopelessness. If emptiness is my "favorite" symptom, hopelessness is undoubtedly my least favorite. It's another symptom that often comes with another well-intended piece of advice that can sometimes be useless: take it one day at a time.

But here's the thing: taking things one day at a time is hell when you have no desire to get to the next day, because you'll just have to fight all over again. It's running on a treadmill that you can't turn off. It's carrying a weight that you can never set down. It's treading water in the middle of the ocean when there's no boat coming to save you[16]. Kind of hard to keep convincing yourself to tread when it's only a matter of time before you ultimately drown. Might as well cut to the chase and not waste energy trying to delay the inevitable.

During a depressive episode, there is no finish line. There is nothing to aim for. There is no light at the end of the tunnel. If you make it through the day, your only "reward" is having to do it all again the next day. If you get through the week, you have to do it all again the next week. Same with months and years. As the famed philosopher Smashmouth once said: "The years start coming and they don't stop coming." I have no science to back this up, but I would bet good money that if you gave this list to everyone who attempted suicide because of depression and asked

---

[16] This isn't a citation, just a fun joke this sentence reminded me of: There was once a drowning man. A boat came by and tried to save him, but he said, "no thank you, God will save me." Another boat tried to save him, but he said, "no thank you, God will save me." Eventually the man drowned. When he got to heaven he asked God, "why didn't you save me?" God answered, "I sent you two boats, you big dummy!"

them to choose which symptom was the straw that broke the camel's back, a distinct majority would point to hopelessness.

Of all the things that are hard to face in regard to hopelessness, the worst of all is how it haunts you. I made it through my first depressive episode, but not without some scars. In the years that followed, every time I felt sad—even if it was for a totally rational reason—I was afraid I wouldn't be happy again. John Green phrased it beautifully in *The Fault in Our Stars*: "There's no way of knowing that your last good day is your Last Good Day. At the time, it is just another good day." Anytime I felt something negative, I was terrified that it would stick and plunge me into months of uncontrollable darkness.

Once you have your first depressive episode, your odds of having a second are dishearteningly high. In a longitudinal study done in 2000, 202 out of 318 subjects who recovered from a first depressive episode suffered a recurrence[17]. That's nearly 65%. If you have a second episode, which officially upgrades you to recurrent major depressive disorder, your odds of a third are even higher. The same study found that the risk of recurrence increased by 16% with each additional recurrence…and that just makes the whole hopeless thing even more infuriating.

For arguments' sake, let's say I can summon the fight to get through a day, a week, a month, or a year. Maybe I can even summon enough fight to get through to the end of the depressive episode. Knowing that each battle I face—regardless of whether I win—makes me even more likely to have another battle…that is a

---

[17] Solomon, D. A. "Multiple Recurrences of Major Depressive Disorder." American Journal of Psychiatry, vol. 157, no. 2, 2000, pp. 229–233., https://doi.org/10.1176/appi.ajp.157.2.229.

tough pill to swallow. At that point, it can be near impossible to rationalize trying to get through the current episode.

Number Two: Loss of interest or pleasure

I'll never forget the first doctor I went to about my depression. Mom dragged me all but kicking and screaming to our local GP. Strike one was the fact that I'd never met this doctor before; I was a few months into being 18 and could no longer go to the pediatrician I'd known for years. We were flying blind and about to hit this poor doctor with "Hi, I'm Sinéad and I have approximately no will to live anymore." Being 18 years old turned out to be strike two, as doctors are pretty hesitant to prescribe antidepressants to teenagers.

Strike three was a knuckleball—a knuckleball that messed me up so bad that it stopped me from seeking medical help for my mental health issues for half a decade. Strike three was when the doctor's professional opinion was that I should try doing things that make me happy. Why didn't I think of that? How could I not put together that watching a marathon of *Glee* episodes would cure my chemically imbalanced brain? Or shooting hoops with friends would make my brain produce enough serotonin that life would feel worth living? Boy, I just feel so grateful to have had that very productive and uplifting appointment with Doctor Useful.

Mom told me years later that she would have paid off that doctor to prescribe jellybeans to me, just to give me any semblance of hope. So, when the doctor produced "try being happy to not be depressed anymore," I think she was lucky that Mom is a graceful woman with plenty of restraint. I genuinely hope that doctor has learned a bit more about mental health in the last few years since then. And if she hasn't…I pray she has moved into an area of medicine where she isn't as much of a risk to derail struggling patients.

Before my first major episode, my favorite things to do were watch *Glee*, play basketball, work out, and play video games. During the episode, I couldn't bring myself to care about a single one of those. The one thing that did make me feel alive was music. I bought a child's guitar no bigger than my quad muscle and taught myself to play. I played for hours on end, picking chords until my fingers bled. I then bought a mini keyboard to hook up to my computer and write my own music.

When my second depressive episode began, I turned to music in the hopes that it would have the same effect. It didn't. That was a diddly darn disappointment. My guitar got buried under layers of dust, I sold my keyboard, and my songwriting journal became nothing more than a deeply emotional coaster. I had free access to the gym at Mom's work, which normally would have been a utopia for me, but I couldn't work up the energy to go, let alone actually exercise. I started watching *The Great British Bake Off*.

None of my previous sources of joy were doing much but spending every Sunday baking and trying out new recipes gave me a taste of happiness (pun very much intended). I also saw an ad to download The Sims 4 for $5; Brianna and I spent countless hours playing The Sims when we were younger, so for five bucks it seemed worth the try. I'm sure a psychologist could do a deep dive into some analysis of me finding control in a simulated world that I couldn't find in my own life, but all that really mattered to me was that time flew by when I was playing.

Even as I consumed heartwarming baking shows or led my Sims to their happy and successful little lives, none of it made me feel much joy. They were pastimes. Nothing more than a tolerable way to take up a few hours of the day as I counted down until it was late enough to go to sleep. Pleasure wasn't in the cards, and my interest in anything was limited, so everything I tried boiled down to the same goal: take up time until the day ends.

I went to work to make the time go by faster. I went to the gym or on walks with Mom to make the time go by faster. I stared at the trees outside my bedroom window, drove unnecessarily far to get food[18], took the long way home, and made no effort to avoid traffic—all in a valiant attempt to make time go by faster.

Number Three: Weight loss or gain

I was a twig before my depressive episode hit and managed to get even twiggier through it. I weighed 145 pounds when it started and crashed down to nearly 130 in two months. For a few weeks, I thought my collar bones were going to tear through my skin because there was so little meat on my bones.

Eating was an unexpected challenge, as it became a nexus of a few different symptoms. I had a hard time making decisions, so even if I was hungry, there was a decent chance I wouldn't eat simply because I couldn't decide what to eat. I had little interest or pleasure in cooking or trying new foods; I recall a week when I ate nothing but Cheerios and eggs because they were easy and got the

---

[18] I went to seven different Five Guys restaurants in the South Bay; the closest was five minutes from my apartment, but that didn't take near enough time. I once considered driving from San Jose to Santa Cruz for an ice cream for no reason other than it would take a really long time.

job done. I had so little energy that the thought of cooking an entire meal for just myself seemed pointlessly daunting. On top of it all, I also had very little appetite. I could prepare a stunning meal with every food I've ever loved, and there was a good chance that after four bites, I'd be full. It would go into the fridge —also known as the black hole of leftovers—eventually get dry and/or moldy, and ultimately find its way to the bottom of the trash can.

It took about eight weeks to lose 10% of my body weight and nearly eight months to gain it back. Working to gain weight is an odd sensation—and something that absolutely no one I interacted with had much sympathy for. I brought my own personal breakfast sandwich maker to work and kept eggs, bacon, Canadian bacon, cheese, and Bagel Thins in the fridge at work. My coworkers liked to tease me about my daily breakfast sammies, but deep down I'm pretty sure they were jealous. Let's just say they walked into the office each morning asking what it was that smelled so good. Point for me.

Number Four: Insomnia or hypersomnia

I'll never not be entertained by the duality that both sleeping too much and not being able to sleep are both on the list for the same illness. It's very emblematic of how contradictory and confusing and overall annoying depression is. I feel lucky that sleep wasn't too much of an issue during my second episode; I was exhausted a lot of the time, but things were pretty normal when I hit the sheets. I guess that's a pinch of hypersomnia, since I spent so much time sleeping. I looked forward to going to bed every night, because it was the one part of the day that wouldn't be miserable. Nothing went wrong in my dreams—since I wasn't really having any dreams—and it was the most harmless way to spend 7–10 hours. I didn't have to feel pain, I didn't have to put on a fake smile, and I didn't have to fight. My mind and body could simply rest.

There was only one night that my determination to sleep was problematic. As was the norm, I was having a bad day. Sad, frustrated, exhausted…the usual. Mom and I texted regularly, and I had told her things weren't going well. I called in sick to work and then proceeded to have a small anxiety attack. It couldn't have been later than maybe 5 p.m., but I told Mom I was exhausted. Remember that "dancing around statements that should have been clearly stated" issue we talked about earlier? Here we go again. When I said I was exhausted, what I meant was, "I am going to sleep." I hit send, climbed into bed, and was out like a light within minutes. Mom did not interpret my text the same way, so when I all of a sudden stopped replying and didn't answer her attempts to call, her mind went to a darker place.

I don't know how long I'd been asleep when I heard my front door rattling. I lived in a studio apartment, so there weren't any walls between the front door, kitchen, living area, and bedroom area. I could see the door, and I could see the outline of a shadow under the door. It rattled again, and in my delirious, half-asleep state, I decided I was about to be robbed. The door shook one more time, and I heard the deadbolt unlock.

I sat up in bed and took a quick inventory around the room. I had a fire extinguisher beside my bed in case of emergencies, and my bedside "table" was a small metal cube/locker kind of thing. I had a box of sports equipment, including a tennis racket, next to a lamp. There were plenty of makeshift weapons within reach that I could use to defend myself from the impending thief. The door opened, and I saw a dark silhouette in the doorway. I leaped out of my bed, not paying a whole lot of attention to which of my various defensive objects I had grabbed. My heart pounded as I bolted towards the closet. No clue why I aimed there. The figure walked through the door and called my name. It was Mom.

The relief that washed over me drained all the coordination from my body as I dropped to the floor, still clutching my weapon of choice. When Mom realized she had scared the living daylights out of me, she joined me on the ground and tried to calm me down. We then both looked at the weapon I'd gone with: Pug, my sister's old stuffed animal from childhood. All I can say is thank God the "robber" was Mom coming to check in on me. If I'd actually had to defend myself, I don't know how effective Pug would have been. He's cute and fluffy and comforting, but not exactly the most ferocious defender.

Number Five: Psychomotor agitation or retardation

Worth noting…DSM-V has a boatload of issues[19], language choice very much included. What they're saying here is that you'll move at the pace of DMV workers on a Friday afternoon after you've been in line for four and a half hours and you just want to get home. It is a strange sensation to seemingly be moving in slow motion. The rest of the world was going at its regular pace, while I was knee-deep in mud. I just couldn't keep up. Everyone else was thinking faster, acting faster, and living faster than I was.

Number Six: Fatigue

---

[19] Homosexuality was in the DSM as a mental illness through the 1970s, suggesting it was a disease that could be cured with the right treatment. Yikes.

I'm lumping number five and number six together because, for me, psychomotor agitation definitely got muddled in with fatigue, and at a certain point it doesn't matter what you call it. Whether it's psychomotor agitation, general fatigue, or a result of insomnia, you're just plain exhausted by the end of the day. Getting out of bed is exhausting. Making food is exhausting. Commuting to work is exhausting. Work itself is exhausting. Every minute of every day is exhausting.

Number Seven: Decreased concentration

Indecisiveness for the win! I'll dive into this more in the meds chapter, but for now, let's briefly touch on decisions I cried over:

- Getting dinner from Chipotle or Five Guys
- Wearing dark shorts with a bright t-shirt and sweater, light shorts with a dark t-shirt and sweater, or dark shorts with a long sleeve—because maybe it won't be that cold and I won't need the sweater and if I have to take off the sweater then I don't want to have to carry it around with me.
- Watching the Super Bowl at my apartment or my parents' house
- Deciding between having taquitos, pizza rolls, chips and guac, or wings during the Super Bowl
- Watching *Stuart Little* or *Cars*
- Keeping my nutcase of a hamster or bringing her back to PetSmart
- Going to my aunt and uncle's for Christmas dinner
- Calling in sick to work
- Buying the Spiderman PS4 video game
- Having Apple Jacks or Corn Pops for breakfast

In hindsight, some of these were hilarious. I stood, crying, butt naked, staring at my closet for a good ten minutes trying to decide what to wear. Another day, I bought enough food for an entire fraternity house to watch the Super Bowl when it was just Mom and me actually eating it. Although, technically speaking, Mom made that decision for me. I called her while having a small panic attack in the frozen food aisle at Safeway, so she told me to buy everything, and we'd figure it out later. I don't think she realized I was bringing home approximately 14,000 calories of food.

Number Eight: Thoughts of death or suicide

Suicide is scary. Having thoughts of suicide, whether they're on the back burner or the front burner, is terrifying. For me, the biggest fear came in hindsight, after the thoughts had passed. It's one thing to be in a place so dark that the pain feels unbearable, but to be a step removed from that darkness and to look back on it can be even worse.

In the interest of full transparency, before I found myself in that darkness, I never understood suicide. I couldn't understand how someone could be in so much pain that death was the only answer. I couldn't fathom how you could be willing to put your loved ones through so much pain. I couldn't understand it until I found myself there. It isn't a desire to die; it's a desperation to stop the daily pain. It isn't a decision made with the intention of hurting loved ones or transferring your pain to others; in the moment, it truly seems like the best choice. Sometimes, it appears to be the only choice.

Depression doesn't just hurt the person with the illness; it also hurts everyone who loves them. I could clearly see how much my family was struggling to support me, and how much it was hurting them to see me in pain. In my eyes, amid the darkness and the worst pain I'd ever felt, I thought killing myself was the best thing for everyone. I knew it would hurt them; hell, I knew it would devastate them. But at least it would be over. They would process their grief and ultimately move on with their lives without me. I'd be a memory rather than a constant source of pain and sadness. I was wrong, and (looking at it from a better place) it's terrifying that my mind could get so muddled that I truly believed my parents' lives would be made better by burying me. It is a parent's worst nightmare, and yet my chemically imbalanced brain led me to believe it was the best choice.

An unexpected side effect of my suicidal ideations was fearlessness. I used to be afraid of darn near everything: heights, the dentist, public speaking, cotton swabs, most movies rated PG-13 or above, and almost every dog in the world[20]. When I started wanting to die, many of those fears dissipated. I went zip lining with Brianna and wasn't scared about the rope snapping or me falling from the sky. I'd be dead, and all my pain would be gone. During a family trip to Hawaii, Brianna and I climbed to the top of a rock overlooking a waterfall lake and took the leap; I wasn't afraid of landing on rocks or being eaten by a piranha. If either of those happened, I'd be dead, and all my pain would be gone.

At its core, fear is a survival instinct. When you no longer have any desire to survive, that instinct starts to get cloudy. I didn't want my body to react to potential threats with self-preservation techniques. If anything, I wanted my body to lean into those threats that much more. I wasn't any sort of adrenaline

---

[20] Shoutout to Lily Rose the Chiweenie, the only dog on planet earth I'm not afraid of.

junkie looking for something to feel alive, and I wouldn't even say I was looking for a convenient way to die. I was just hoping death would happen to cross my path and take care of business.

Bottom line, the DSM-5 requires that patients exhibit five symptoms to be considered depressed. I obliterated that glass ceiling and ticked every single box over the course of my entire episode. My sister always used to be the "above and beyond" kid, but I easily have her beat on this one. Nine for nine, baby!

Talking About Feelings

I have a long history with therapists. The first time I was in therapy was when I was three years old. I don't remember it, but I don't doubt it. I was known to have meltdowns in parking lots when it was time to choose whether to drive home with Mom or Dad...even though they were both going to the same place...at the same time. It appears I've been a hot mess since the moment I exited the womb.

Fast-forwarding to high school, I went to the first therapist I actually remember. I was a few weeks into freshman year and having a rough time adjusting—so rough that after day one I started researching how to transfer to a different high school in the district. Mom found a therapist, and I willingly went to the first appointment. I did not like it one bit. I realize that the problems I was presenting (I go to Hillsdale, my best friends go to Aragon. My friends at Hillsdale aren't in my classes...and that's about it) weren't necessarily of the same caliber the therapist was probably used to, but to me they were world-stopping. She made no effort to hide how small she thought my problems were.

After one appointment, I begged Mom to let me bail on the following three appointments. Mom tried to cancel, but the therapist essentially didn't let her. She said it was "important that I follow through with therapy." I have a hunch it was more important that she got paid for three more sessions, but maybe I'm just cynical. In any sense, Mom bribed me with cookies and ice cream to power through the other three sessions, and I never saw that therapist again.

Next up is Greg. In my sophomore year of high school, a disgruntled former student decided that the best way to manage his complex feelings was by storming campus on a Monday morning with pipe bombs, a chainsaw, and a samurai sword. By the grace of God—and the grace of the punk's incompetence—nobody got hurt. But being on lockdown for who knows how long, not knowing if my family were safe, dealing with a mess of communication trying to understand what was happening, and waiting for the bomb squad to escort us off campus took a major toll on my mental health. Not entirely surprising. I spoke with the counselors the school brought in to help us all in the first few days following the attack, but once they all went back to their day jobs it became clear that I needed a little bit more support. The Youth Services Bureau (A+ program, 10/10 would recommend) connected me with a therapist I could meet with weekly until my mental and emotional state improved. Mom and Dad were skeptical at first, since Greg was still in his training hours and wasn't a fully "official" therapist at the time, but I truly do not know where I'd be without him. We worked through the PTSD symptoms I was feeling from the attack, but also started to dive into some other aspects of my life I hadn't been as aware needed support. When basketball season got underway, my sessions with Greg fizzled, but he got me through the toughest time of my life, and for that, I will always be grateful.

The therapist journey was one of peaks and valleys. Greg was a peak—probably the ultimate peak. Next up, though, came the biggest valley. Simply put, this woman should not be allowed to work in healthcare, let alone mental health, ever again.

Let's set the scene: it's October 2012, and I have been at the University of Oregon for a few weeks. It is not going well. I knew Greg had been helpful for me, so I had faith in the general concept of therapy. I made an appointment with the University health center's counseling department, answered all of their screening questions honestly, and headed in to talk with a counselor. It was a forty-minute appointment, and the only thing I've seen crash faster in forty minutes is Gonzaga's 2021 Men's Basketball National Championship dreams against Baylor[21].

The first ten minutes were par for the course: I kept my emotions in check as I tried to articulate what I was feeling and thinking in general terms. Then the therapist asked if I'd had any suicidal thoughts, and I had to take a pause. The truth was, yes, those thoughts had started creeping into my head. I didn't know at the time that when you say "yes" to that one question, you're opening a can of worms you can't possibly close. All of a sudden, you're a red alert, top-level concern.

When I finally admitted to it, the floodgates opened. I felt like I was really connecting with the therapist, and I felt safe and comfortable letting everything out; every fear swirling hopelessly

---

[21] It still hurts to think about. THAT WAS THE TEAM. THAT WAS THE SEASON. IT WAS MEANT TO BE…until it wasn't.

around my head, every thought that had been scaring me, every new feeling I didn't know what to do with. When my monologue ended, I felt a fleeting moment of relief. I felt like maybe, just maybe, this woman could help me like Greg had. She paused, then reached into her desk. I thought she was getting her schedule out so we could pencil in some regular sessions, but that wasn't the case. Instead, she pulled out a pile of brochures, pamphlets, and business cards for other therapists around town. Then she hit me with two sentences that rocked me to my core: "It sounds like you're really struggling, but I think it is more than what we are equipped to handle. You should look into getting some help from a professional in the community."

And that was it. I was a wee little freshman, overwhelmed by every aspect of my life, falling apart inside, and screaming for help, only to be told that I was too messed up for them to even try to fix. It had taken a lot out of me just to make that first appointment—there was no way that I was going to call half a dozen random therapists in a state I'd lived in for less than four weeks. I didn't know if insurance would help or if I would have to pay out of pocket. I didn't know if I was going to get swept to the looney bin if I told anyone else what I was feeling—and I absolutely was not ready to find out. I continued suffering in silence for another six weeks through the end of the term and then dropped out.

When I got back home, it seemed obvious that I should see a therapist—one who was "equipped to handle" whatever I was dealing with. I don't want to say it was PTSD, but I definitely had some trauma to unpack after the Oregon "therapy" incident. I hesitate even to call it therapy because it was so catastrophic. In less than an hour, my trust for the entire concept of therapy and the industry of mental health professionals had been all but shattered—with only one exception. Greg.

W hen I had worked with Greg after the bombing, there was a clear trigger and a rational reason for everything I was feeling. We had the dots on a page and just needed to connect them. The second time, I don't even know what we had in front of us. Crumpled up construction paper and some melted crayons? In the three years since my first time working with Greg, he had become an "official" therapist and started his own practice in the East Bay. Every Tuesday, after finishing class at the local community college, I'd drive the forty-five minutes out to Lafayette. We'd work for an hour straight—I usually had a headache by the time we finished just from focusing so hard— then I'd stop by Noah's Bagels for a chocolate chip bagel and drive the hour or so back home (hooray for Bay Area traffic!).

One of my favorite things about working with Greg was how un-therapist-y he is. He auditioned for *American Ninja Warrior*, which already made him the most badass therapist on the planet. Beyond that, he also wasn't above some good old-fashioned incentives: in particular, Three Twins chocolate ice cream. He sent me home from each session with homework, whether it was readings, journaling, reflections, observations, or anything else. So long as I came back the following week with the work done, he showed up with a fresh pint of Three Twins. Let me be clear: Three Twins is phenomenal ice cream. I'm a bit of an ice cream aficionado, and Three Twins is one of the best. Smooth, strong flavor, creamy…it's sheer perfection.

Besides the fact that he gave me ice cream, what I appreciated the most about Greg was how hard he made me work. If I was going to schlep out to the East Bay, I wanted it to be worth it. I wanted to get better. I wanted my life back. And he understood that.

We worked with a therapeutic model called Internal Family Systems, or IFS. IFS is a model created by Richard Schwarz, founded on the premise that we all have parts within ourselves that serve different purposes and have different goals and motivations[22]. The parts also have different levels of maturity, experience, pain, and everything else. In essence, they are their own micro-personality. Every part is valuable, so long as it exists in a healthy role. When parts can't stay in their lane and start to exist in "extreme roles," things get a little out of whack.

I'll admit, I was skeptical when Greg first suggested it. It seemed like he was trying to make me a controlled schizophrenic by encouraging me to find little voices in my head, but the more I bought in and the deeper I dove into IFS, the more powerful it became. Our parts work in three roles: managers, exiles, and firefighters. Manager parts protect us and prevent pain from reaching the Self. Exile parts are those that we often try to bury and shield from the Self, usually formative moments from childhood. Firefighter parts, much like real-life firefighters, come in times of emergency. Underneath all the parts is the Self. When parts get out of order and fall into extreme roles, it gets the Self all tangled up. IFS is about connecting with each part, listening to the part, understanding the part, and trying to guide the part back to its healthy role.

---

[22] Schwartz, Richard. Introduction to the Internal Family Systems Model. Trailheads Publications, 2001.

Time flew by when I was working with my parts. Hourlong sessions would go by in an instant. Some weeks I would discover new parts; other weeks, we would try to connect deeper with a part who had shown up in a more extreme role. But every week, I edged closer and closer to getting the steering wheel back in the Self's hands. The strategies I learned not only helped get me through that crisis but also allowed me to understand nuances about myself I'd never before acknowledged.

I worked with Greg for close to a year, and by the time we tapered off our sessions, he had truly given me my life back. He swears it was all my hard work that allowed me to regain control, but without his direction, I don't think I ever would have gotten there.

The last therapist in my Rolodex is Lisa. When my second major depressive episode began and I finally accepted that I needed help, the natural choice would have been to go back to Greg. Unfortunately, he had since moved out of state with his wife. I found Lisa online—she worked in the same building as my new psychiatrist, and she seemed nice enough—so I went with her. She was perfectly fine but didn't have the same level of attack that Greg had. Greg had a game plan each time I walked through the door. Even if I wanted to make small talk, it never lasted for more than a minute or two. We had work to do, and he was going to make the most of every minute we had.

With Lisa, I was supposed to take the lead. I'd arrive for my appointment, and she'd ask what I wanted to work on or talk about. I never knew what to say because I never felt comfortable enough to just hit her with the deep stuff straight off the bat. I didn't know if she wanted surface-level context before diving in, or if she wanted to cannonball straight into the deep end. As a result, it ended up feeling like I was paying a fat chunk of change to make small talk with an unremarkable lady once a week, and I certainly wasn't making any measurable therapeutic progress. In my eyes, I'd come to terms with everything: my brain was fundamentally, chemically messed up; it wasn't my fault; I couldn't have done anything to prevent it; all that needed to be done was to get the meds figured out to recalibrate my natural happy juices.

Should I go back to therapy to unpack everything else a bit more? Probably. But if I'm being completely honest, it's hard to imagine working with anyone other than Greg, let alone making as much progress with anyone else as I did with Greg. But if any of y'all know of any Ninja Warrior therapists in the Bay Area who will give me ice cream...feel free to send their info my way.

Intermission #1
"Inside Out" Is the Most Important Movie Ever Made

As I mentioned earlier, Internal Family Systems was the most successful therapeutic approach for me, but it can be incredibly difficult to explain without it sounding like schizophrenia. Describing your true Self as a sum of various "parts," each of which has different ages, experiences, roles, and identities, is admittedly abnormal. I tried sending my family articles, videos, and interviews with Richard Schwarz to help them understand, but we didn't get very far. Then Disney Pixar's *Inside Out* came out, and all of a sudden, the entire model of IFS became approachable, digestible, endearing, and ultimately, understandable.

Disney allowed people to develop compassion for what Riley (the main character) is dealing with and even compassion for each of Riley's parts. They let people see that you do need to have anger, disgust, and sadness. Being only happy all the time doesn't work and isn't even fundamentally accurate. You find yourself rooting for each part to show up when it's their time to shine and hoping that all of the parts will find a way to work in synchronization with one another to help Riley adjust to her major life changes. You see how her childhood experiences have introduced and affected her parts, and how some of those memories crumble when her parts begin to exist in extreme roles.

In recent years, representation in mass media has become a much more visible issue. People always talk about how important it is to have representation of all genders, races, sexualities, identities, and so much more, and *Inside Out* is the first time I really felt that. As a white woman, there's plenty of representation of my race and growing representation of my gender expression. But as a completely high functioning, normal-presenting, everyday person battling daily with mental illness, *Inside Out* was the first time I felt truly seen and understood.

When you think about movies about mental health, your mind usually goes to films like *One Flew Over the Cuckoo's Nest*, *Rain Man*, *Radio*, or A *Beautiful Mind*. While those movies have plenty of characters with mental illnesses, they never explored the innermost workings of the mind. *Inside Out* does that. So, if you haven't seen it, stick a bookmark on this page and use this intermission to watch it. You won't regret it.

Alrighty, we're back. Great movie, innit?

Happy Pills

Antidepressants are rude. Just plain rude. I get that side effects are unavoidable, and I get that when you're working with the madness that is the human brain, things can get weird. But good Lord, it's just plain offensive that before you get to the meds cocktail that actually sorts you out, you basically end up in a way less fun human version of Super Mario Bros. You have to keep battling new beasts and opponents and challenges on your way to the magical castle at the end: the right combination of meds.

A large part of why I was so hesitant to try antidepressants was because of all the side effects. It can be tough to wrap your head around *you might be agitated or have no sex drive, have diarrhea or constipation, have insomnia or be totally exhausted, have no appetite or have major weight gain, be super sweaty or have a dry mouth, want to kill yourself even more than when you first started, and also maybe have some kidney function issues or heart rhythm problems…but you won't be depressed anymore! Probably! But no guarantees! You can't quote me on this!* Kind of a raw deal, don't ya think? I mean, I'm already depressed as hell, and that fun menu of bodily chaos doesn't really inspire a whole lot of confidence that the "after" will be much better than the "before."

In the world of antidepressants, you've got a few main categories: selective serotonin reuptake inhibitors (SSRIs), serotonin and norepinephrine reuptake inhibitors (SNRIs), and atypical antidepressants. Serotonin and norepinephrine are neurotransmitters in the brain (little chemical messengers). The way SSRI and SNRIs work (as far as I understand it) is that by blocking the respective neurotransmitter from being reabsorbed back into the nerve that released it, it keeps the little messenger in between two nerve cells for longer[23]. That's the extent of what I understand, and I don't really know how keeping those little messengers in the intersection for longer helps, but if you want the science of it, there is plenty of it online.

The first antidepressant my general practitioner prescribed was Zoloft, a very common SSRI. It's a particular brand of sertraline[24] and, apparently, is par for the course to get the antidepressant ball rolling with a low dose. Within 24 hours of starting Zoloft, things got really weird, really fast. One critically unfortunate detail about the antidepressant prescribing process is that it's basically just a whole lot of guessing and checking. Different meds work for different people, but you've got to give them enough time to settle in before you can fully evaluate if they're working. In my case, when Zoloft started going crazy

---

[23] "SSRI's vs SNRI's - What's the Difference between Them?" Drugs.Com, 13 July 2021, www.drugs.com/medical-answers/difference-between-ssris-snris-3504539.

[24] "Zoloft." Drugs.Com, 7 July 2021, www.drugs.com/zoloft.html.

within 24 hours of my first dose, the only thing we could do was ride it out to see if it would sort itself out. (Spoiler alert: It did not sort itself out. At all.)

After prescribing Zoloft, the doctor had sent me home with a massive stack of informational paperwork, including a list of potential side effects. I think my body interpreted it more as a checklist of challenges and decided to try to achieve every last one of them.

- Sleepiness, drowsiness, tired feeling: I was already exhausted, so this wasn't much of a change. No improvement, but also no worse than beforehand.
- Nervousness, anxiety: The doctor also gave me some Xanax to handle these side effects, but the Xanax had its own set of side effects as well—mostly just knocking me out absolutely cold for twelve or more hours at a time. I had a hard time separating what nervousness and anxiety were a side effect of the Zoloft, versus the general nervousness and anxiety I felt towards starting to take antidepressants.
- Insomnia: So much fun when combined with drowsiness. An absolute blast. Good thing the Xanax turned me into a depressed Sleeping Beauty.
- Dizziness: I don't know if you've ever put your forehead on a bat and spun around a few times, but every so often I'd get hit with a random dizzy spell that felt an awful lot like that. A few of them hit during basketball practice, and those were really fun. I had to hedge my bets a bit when shooting the basketball, hoping I was aiming at the correct rim of the three circling in my field of vision.
- Nausea, upset stomach, stomach pain: This was a strange set of feelings. The nausea was unaffected by anything going on

with my diet; I could be starving, full, in between meals, or just finished eating, and nausea would do its own thing. Never ended up tossing my cookies; I just felt like I might for weeks on end. I have a feeling this may have contributed to the amount of weight I lost.

• Headache: No bueno. Really no bueno when coaching basketball. Extra no bueno when working at a high school. Super-duper no bueno when coaching basketball with players who like to talk really, really loudly all the time.

As an added bonus, I also got some side effects that weren't even on the original list! Memory loss? Yup. General anger and rage? Oof...yes. Crippling indecision? Every minute of every day. I made the mistake of buying a multi-pack of small cereal boxes and ended up crying for 20 minutes one morning because I couldn't decide between Apple Jacks and Corn Pops.

Beyond the standard side effects, I also got hit with an extra special side effect with even more oomph: akathisia. Akathisia is widely known as "restless depression," but I have to say, that's a pretty wild understatement for what it actually feels like[25]. It's a movement disorder often seen as a side effect of antipsychotic drugs, but the medical field hasn't yet figured out why it happens. The leading theory is that the medication may block dopamine, which helps your brain communicate and plays a critical role in muscle control. There are four main types of akathisia, all time-based: acute, which appears as soon as you start taking a medication; chronic, which lasts more than six months;

---

[25] Oghoteru Tachere, Richardson, and Mandana Modirrousta. "Beyond Anxiety and Agitation: A Clinical Approach to Akathisia." Australian Family Physician, vol. 46, no. 5, 2017, pp. 296–98.

tardive, which shows up months or years after taking a medication; and withdrawal, which shows up one to two months after you stop taking a given medication.

I started with acute akathisia, since it showed up almost instantly. Every atom in my body had a mind of its own and was trying to jump out of my skin. It felt like the Energizer Bunny and Taz from the Looney Tunes had a child, and then that child went trick-or-treating, so now they're all hopped up on sugar but haven't started to crash yet.

Simply stated, I was physically incapable of being still. If I was standing, my knees rocked back and forth. While sitting, my right leg bounced like a drummer keeping time with the world's fastest song, at times also joined by the left leg. I could clock thousands of steps each day without leaving my apartment solely from pacing wall to wall. If I was sitting in the backseat of the car and we stopped at a red light, the whole car would shake. Dad thought there was something wrong with the transmission the first few times it happened before we realized it was just my bouncing legs. Hand tremors were a daily occurrence, made worse whenever I tried to calm them. My fine motor skills were a bit of a mess; before one basketball game, I had to ask one of my players to write our roster in the scorebook because my hands were shaking too much for me to do it.

Beyond the physical manifestations, I also felt like I was just plain losing my mind. It felt like a treadmill going at top speed, or like someone was hitting fast forward on my life, and I couldn't keep up. My thoughts bounced all over the place, and nothing made sense. My breathing was short, my heart raced, and every day I thought I might just explode with all the energy pulsing through my veins. The depression had already taken control of my mind, and the akathisia was taking my body. There was nothing left in me that I could actually control. Say what you will about waterboarding or posting seventh-grade school photos on the internet, but taking away a person's control of their mind and body might just be the cruelest form of torture there is. And all along the way, the only attempts at relief I got were reminders that if I stuck through it, things would probably get better.

My depressive episode started in August 2018, and the Zoloft escapade began in early November 2018. By Thanksgiving, things were still getting progressively worse. A friend had given me a pair of tickets to the Golden State Warriors game the day before Thanksgiving, and I invited Brianna to join me. Pies are kind of my thing, so my job for Thanksgiving was baking two pies for the family, and a third for a family friend. Not too much on my plate, right? Wrong. Absolutely wrong.

On the Wednesday, I woke before 6 a.m., already feeling some anxiety about the game. How would we get there? Drive? Take BART? Where would we get on BART? Would we get dinner before? At the arena? At the Denny's across from the arena? If we got food, would we eat it on BART? Did I need to pick up Brianna? Would she meet me there? How would we deal with having two cars? How much did parking cost? Would we be able to find nearby parking that would be more affordable? If we did park farther away, would our cars be safe?

I spent between four and five hours pacing in circles, working myself into a full tizzy thinking about Warrior game logistics. And then it hit me: I had to make three pies the next day. Forget just a tizzy; it was time for a full-blown anxiety attack. I called Mom to let her know I couldn't possibly go to the game because I had too much else to deal with. My brain couldn't handle multi-step processes and reacted by going into complete and utter panic mode. Big kudos to Mom for talking me through what I'm sure was a laughable crisis on her end. I mean, come on…a Warrior game and baking pies? With a stable brain, that sounds like an awesome forty-eight hours—seriously, sign me up! She wrote out a timeline for the day, broke down all the steps, and planned who would help me on each one, simplifying the day to the point that I had some confidence I could make it through.

I know I survived Thanksgiving, as it has come and gone, but I am left with very little recollection of that time. I remember some of the major traumas, but the first few Zoloft months really didn't stick in my memory. I don't know if I'm blocking them out because they were so dark, or if something with my brain chemistry prevented me from forming the memories. I just know that I barely remember that Thanksgiving. I know I was coaching basketball that year, but I couldn't tell you much more than maybe half of the girls' names and a couple of the most dramatic points of the season. I don't remember what else I was working on, or anything else I was doing. Like dish soap on a slip 'n slide, the memories just didn't stick.

Fast forward a couple of weeks, and my patience for Zoloft was rapidly running out. I had given it the requisite time to "settle in," and all it had done was turn me into a walking earthquake actively losing her marbles. It was time to get the meds adjusted, but I couldn't get in to see my regular doctor. Mom was able to get me an appointment at a different clinic, but it turns out that getting a prescription adjusted is not as easy as walking in and asking any old doctor to make some changes. We also happened to get particularly unlucky with the doctor who was on call. I got the sense that she was relatively new, and maybe didn't have time to read my file before she walked in, but in any sense, I rocked her boat pretty badly as soon as she started asking questions.

> Doc: How are we today?
>
> Me: My medications are not working, and I would like the dosage adjusted or them changed altogether or something.
>
> Doc: Okay, have you been having any trouble sleeping?
>
> Me: Yep
>
> Doc: How is your appetite?
>
> Me: Not very good. I also can't stop shaking.
>
> Doc: And how is your pee pee?
>
> Me: What?
>
> Doc: Your pee pee. Is going to the bathroom okay?
>
> Me: Oh, yeah. It's fine.
>
> Doc: Do you ever have thoughts of harming yourself?
>
> Me: Yep
>
> Doc: *starting to show signs of fluster* How often?
>
> Me: Probably every day, but it's just kind of in the back of my mind.
>
> Doc: *very flustered* I'll be right back.

She returned ten minutes later and said that I needed to go to the mental health clinic a few blocks away. She also told Mom that we should stop by McDonald's on the way to get breakfast and that they had a drive-through! Kind of an odd suggestion, but I think the poor lady just wanted to get me out of her office before I offed myself on the spot.

It turned out that the mental health "clinic" was actually mental health "urgent care." Critical detail. And boy oh boy, mental health urgent care is no joke. I may be a crazy, but these were some next-level crazies. I wouldn't be surprised if they had straitjackets in the back, locked and loaded should the need arise. As soon as we walked in and saw a police officer posted at the door and a lady talking to a chair, Mom and I knew we were in for a wild ride.

I checked in, and half an hour later I got in to see the first person. I don't actually know if she was a nurse, therapist, case manager, or psychiatrist. There were many titles for many different people, and I couldn't keep them straight. I gave her the same rundown about my medication issues and asked if she could make some adjustments. She nodded nicely, thankfully didn't ask about my pee pee, and asked me to take a seat in the waiting room until I could see a case manager. The lady talking to a chair moved to start chatting with a picture frame as we sat down to wait.

Another half hour came and went before we got in to see the case manager. She was another very nice lady; I gave her the same rundown I had now told to three different people in the span of ninety minutes, and she finally gave us the very useful piece of information (that would have been great to know an hour or so earlier) that the only person who can change my prescription is the original prescribing doctor. The only other option was to be admitted to the hospital, which would then allow a psychiatrist to adjust my meds.

Now that may seem simple enough…get admitted, meet with a psychiatrist, get some things switched up, and be on my merry way. The only problem is that if you get admitted from mental health urgent care after telling three people in the span of ninety minutes that you regularly think about ending your life, it isn't a regular old hospital admittance. It's a full-blown 5150—a seventy-two-hour involuntary hold. To be honest, I would have been okay with it, but I had basketball practice to coach that afternoon, and I hadn't exactly told my bosses what had been going on with my noggin. I wasn't sure how well a voicemail from Mom was going to be received: "Hi, this is Sinéad's mom. She'll have to miss practice today, and probably the next two days because she is currently locked in a straitjacket in the looney bin. But don't worry, she's probably fine and she'll be back on Thursday! Thanks!"

Mom and I said thanks but no thanks, and that we'd find another way to sort things out. We got sent back to the waiting room to wait for a psychiatrist to check in with. I have to say, of all the flaws in the US healthcare system, an incredibly underrated one is how difficult it is to discern required treatment, recommended treatment, optional treatment, and what could potentially get me 5150-ed. I know that, theoretically, I am in charge of all of my medical decisions, but it is awfully hard to figure out how to exercise those rights.

Yet another half hour passed us by, and the psychiatrist was still nowhere to be seen. Mom decided that we were done and that it was time to bust out of there. I went up to the receptionist, asked for my discharge paperwork, and declined further care. She looked at me with a lot of concern and very little trust in her eyes, but ultimately let me leave. I got a little nervous that the cop was going to follow us out and march me back in—a coincidentally timed siren as we reached the parking lot added to the nerves—but Mom and I successfully got the hell out of there…still with the same prescription and still with the same madness of Zoloft.

I finally got in to see my regular doctor, a sweet woman with the best of intentions, but by that point she was wildly out of her depth with me. She tried adding a small dose of Wellbutrin to the mix, but it didn't do much. General practitioners have so many skills, but when it comes to the nuance of antidepressants, you need to bring in a specialist…which we didn't know was a separate thing until after Christmas.

On January 9, I got in to see psychiatrist Dr. Montez, and it didn't take her more than a minute and a half to see that I was a hot mess. The akathisia was still going full steam ahead, and despite all the side effects, I still wasn't seeing any of the intended benefits from the medication. Straight off the bat, she took me off Zoloft.

I thought eliminating the cause of the akathisia would, in turn, eliminate the akathisia itself. As it turned out, that isn't always how it plays out. Which, again, is a pretty raw deal (even more evidence that antidepressants are assholes). For most people, the symptoms will fade when the medications are changed—but for a select few of us, we get to keep our bouncy legs even after making adjustments to our dosages. Some of us really lucky ducks get to keep the bouncy legs forever! Hooray! A solid six months later, I was still so shaky that pitching a summer camp Wiffle ball game turned into me launching Wiffle balls to the moon, inadvertently beaning ten-year-olds and getting heckled by second graders. Over the last year, I've been working on paint by numbers—partially as a mindless stress reliever, and partially to work on finding ways to regain control over my fine motor skills. I like to think I'm improving, but every so often I'll have a spontaneous, excessively shaky day for no apparent reason.

I started on Zoloft, and I think we can safely put that down as a failed first attempt. The regular doctor added Wellbutrin, and things got marginally better, but it didn't make enough of a difference. Wellbutrin is the brand name for bupropion, a norepinephrine-dopamine reuptake inhibitor (NDRI). Bupropion is also used for people with seasonal affective disorder (which has the most fitting acronym in the history of acronyms...SAD), with ADHD, or to help people quit smoking. It's like the Meryl Streep of drugs—unbelievable range. Seizures are a major potential side effect; thankfully, I didn't have any of those. In fact, the transition to bupropion was probably the smoothest. I don't know if everything felt easier because it was coming on the heels of the Zoloft-triggered akathisia, or if I actually didn't have as many side effects. I got a little sweaty and continued to lose weight, but it was nothing compared to all the residual issues from Zoloft.

Dr. Montez got rid of Zoloft, which was another step in the right direction, but it still wasn't enough. She doubled the Wellbutrin dosage; still not enough. A distinct majority of my side effects were physical, but the few mental ones were undoubtedly the hardest ones to handle. I still struggled with decision-making, and my emotions were all over the place. In March, Mom and I went to a basketball game. I didn't get to a concession stand before it closed, so I couldn't get an ice cream cone, and it sent me into a three-day spiral of rage, frustration, and sadness. Over one insignificant little ice cream cone.

Best of all, my memory was starting to get out of whack. I could forget anything from a single conversation to an entire week. If I made plans with anyone, I had to write it in my planner and schedule it in my phone immediately, or I'd likely forget the conversation ever happened. Pro Tip: Mini notepads are a godsend for memory issues. I had a two-inch spiral-bound notepad I kept with me at all times, and I wrote down absolutely everything. Before introducing myself to a large group, I wrote down everything I'd need to say: my name, where I went to school, my hometown, and a fun fact. I had to write down arrival and dismissal times for work, and darn near everything anyone said to me throughout the day. My memory was so sporadic that I couldn't take a chance on banking on remembering anything—and when I say I forgot, I mean it was completely wiped from my brain. No fuzzy recollection, no déjà vu, no vague sense of the conversation. It was entirely blank.

Dr. Montez then added in Lexapro, a brand name SSRI for escitalopram. Again, things got a little better. But again, it wasn't enough. That was when I started feeling just plain stupid, which wasn't even on the list of side effects. I think it's a spin-off side effect from the memory issues, but I can't be sure. Mid-conversation, even mid-sentence, I would forget a word and come to a screeching halt at that word. I couldn't pull out a synonym or any sort of description of the word, but I also couldn't move past it in a sentence. They wouldn't even be complex words; key, elevator, nursing, or book. It would turn into a tragic one-way game of charades with me helplessly miming and stammering "the…the…um…the…um" until somebody could pull my word out of thin air or continue the conversation without me.

Now, about two years later, the words have sorted themselves out…in exchange for not being able to do math. I'm starting to understand how the Little Mermaid felt when she made a deal with Ursula: she traded her voice for legs; I've exchanged being able to do third-grade math for being able to put together coherent sentences. The difference is, Ariel had a choice. I got dealt this hand with zero input on my end.

If someone asked you what two plus two was, you wouldn't have to think about it. Your brain would tell you it was four, and your brain would be right. My brain would, with equal confidence as your brain told you four, tell me five. Or three. Or seven. I once did some quick mental math while on a walk with Mom: 16 times 6. Boom boom quick math, my brain, with complete confidence, told me it was 84. Turns out, it's not. It's 96. I'm not even flipping numbers or being off by some standard unit...my brain is pulling completely random numbers out of thin air. I might as well be rolling dice and going with whatever it lands on. Bottom line, I can't always count on basic arithmetic working for me — pun completely intended. I do my best to laugh it off because that's easier than getting frustrated that I sporadically have the multiplication skills of a six-year-old, but feeling like your brain just doesn't work properly is unbearably humbling.

To combat my linguistic incompetence, Dr. Montez decreased Lexapro and added Trintellix, another SSRI. No significant emotional improvement, but my sweat glands went absolutely bananas. You ain't never seen someone as sweaty as me on a hot summer day, running around sports camp. I would bring two or three extra shirts to work each day, so I could change when I sweat through them. I invested in special cooling towels and hats to try to control my body temperature. I started drinking a full gallon of water every day to counteract the amount of water I was sweating out.

New frustrations arose with each unsuccessful adjustment, and with the number of different meds I was on, my risk of developing serotonin syndrome was steadily rising alongside. That's right...you can swing too far in the *other* direction and end up with a whole new kind of sick. Serotonin syndrome, a result of excessive serotonin buildup in the body, has a ridiculously fast onset. More than half of cases show up within six hours, and almost all cases happen within twenty-four hours. If it isn't treated quickly and properly, it can be deadly…and honestly, how messed up is that? Serotonin deficiency makes me suicidal, and now you're telling me that extra serotonin will also kill me? I can't win! Milder cases can be treated by simply stopping whatever medication put you over the edge, while the most severe cases can be fatal[26].

The Mayo Clinic provides a list of fourteen drugs and supplements that can potentially cause serotonin syndrome; of the fourteen, I regularly took three and occasionally used three more. Fun fact of the day: nutmeg can cause serotonin syndrome! Who knew my delicious Thanksgiving apple pies could be weaponized?

After a few weeks of sweating, having the IQ of an eggplant, and still being sad, Dr. Montez nixed the Trintellix and again upped the Lexapro dosage. The serotonin syndrome risk factors were piling up, so I had to be even more aware of my body's reactions, but the emotional progress was worth it. I was finally feeling different—and better. I could tell we were getting close to the magical recipe of happiness, but I was still experiencing too many spikes and crashes to call it a success. The last thing Dr. Montez added was lithium, a mood stabilizer. Finally, after nearly nine months of trial and error, we had hit the right balance. My white blood cell count is a bit low, I have to get regular bloodwork to make sure the lithium isn't doing too much

[26] "Serotonin Syndrome." Mayo Clinic, Mayo Foundation for Medical Education and Research, 10 Dec. 2019, https://www.mayoclinic.org/diseases-conditions/serotonin-syndrome/symptoms-causes/syc-20354758.

to hurt my kidney and liver function, I can't take any NSAIDs[27], and I have to be absurdly hydrated to compensate for the sweatiness and keep the internal organs running properly—but we finally got to that magical, right combination.

I couldn't find a way to naturally weave in my next Pro Tip, but here it is: If insurance isn't covering your medication, use GoodRx and shop around. It's truly disgusting how arbitrary pricing is when it comes to medications. Here's a fun math problem to shine a light on the absurdity of it all. My current prescribed dosage for generic bupropion XL is 450mg. If I were to pay out of pocket for a one-month supply of 450mg tablets at Walgreens, it would cost me $504. With the free coupon from GoodRx, it's $190. But wait—the absurdity continues! At the same Walgreens, I could buy a one-month supply of 150mg tablets for $83 and a one-month supply of 300mg tablets for $112. The exact same amount of medication, for $195 instead of $504. Throw in the GoodRx coupons, and we're down to $37 for the 150mg tablets and $36 for the 300mg tablets. Grand total of $73 instead of $504— and Walgreens wasn't even the cheapest option. At Costco, it would be a total of $24 for a month of 150mg tablets and 300mg tablets.

---

[27] NSAID = non-steroidal anti-inflammatory drug. Super common class of anti-inflammatory medications. Ibuprofen and naproxen are the most well-known NSAIDs and are often the go-to for pain relief. I have a medical bracelet with my current prescriptions, as well as a specific to let any emergency responders know that I am an exclusively acetaminophen woman!

FOR 90 TABLETS OF 300MG BUPROPION XL

	Retail Name Brand	Retail Generic	With Coupon GoodRx
Safeway	$6,932.00	$226.00	$30.12
CVS Pharmacy	$7,390.00	$271.00	$92.50
Walgreens	$8,002.00	$325.00	$98.65
Costco	$6,810.00	$69.00	$26.99
Rite Aid	$7,422.00	$424.00	$61.80
Walmart	$6,894.00	$204.00	$32.49
Target	$7,390.00	$350.00	$92.50
Lucky Pharmacy	$7,422.00	$505.00	$32.84
Ralph's	$7,422.00	$246.00	$18.65
Community	$7,422.00	$346.00	$98.65
Average	$7,310.60	$296.60	$58.52

I'm not sponsored by GoodRx or anything, but their site is an absolute godsend. Dr. Montez recommended it to me after I started a new job and had to change my health insurance. She was no longer in-network, but it didn't seem like a bright idea to start over with a brand-new psychiatrist while also starting a new job, so I decided to take the financial hit and pay out of pocket for her services and my prescriptions. Without the GoodRx coupons, it would have had a much bigger impact on my finances.

Seeing Red

Taylor Swift has an absolutely stunning album called *Red*. I could spend months telling you about all the beautiful intricacies and delicate nuances of the album, but that's a whole other book and not super on topic. What is on topic, though, is colors. I was lucky enough to see Taylor on tour when she performed her *Red* album, and she had a wonderful speech about colors. Here it is:

"The way I see emotion, I kind of compare them to colors. For me, blue is sad. To me, yellow and gold is comfort and warmth. But there's one color that defines a lot of the emotions that I've been writing about lately; really great emotions like frustration, anger, jealousy, falling in love, falling out of love, heartbreak, and all that good stuff…I read about that stuff so much that I even named an entire album after it, and I even went so far as to name an entire world tour after it. Because, ladies and gentlemen, boys and girls, colors define the emotions that shape us and teach us things. I think there's one color that represents the most important ones. And that color is Red."

Ooof. Gives me chills every time. You should pull up the video of it on YouTube to get the full effect. Gosh, I love Taylor. But anyway, let's talk about colors. I think the colors of depression are muted: grey, dark grey, maybe some greyish blue. They have no sparkle, and they're a little out of focus. They are blurry, uninspiring, and altogether dreary. For me, though, I occasionally got a touch of one other color: red. Frustration, anger, jealousy, and heartbreak. Red.

Reds were the feelings I wanted to avoid. It was Red that made me prefer emptiness to sadness. It was Red that made the days I felt nothing the best days. Red was vicious, violent, uncontrollable rage. Red was dangerous. The times when I started to seriously consider attempting suicide weren't because of overwhelming dark grey feelings. They were because of Red feelings.

I was so frustrated with my demented brain that I couldn't fix no matter how hard I tried. I was furious with God and the world for making me this way. I felt burning jealousy for everyone who got to live with the blissful ignorance and delightful simplicity of being neurotypical. I felt heartbroken for the pain I was bringing to my family and the coworkers I was letting down on a daily basis. I had never hated anything as much as I hated myself when I felt Red. The pain that came with Red was the unbearable pain, and the one part I worked hardest to control.

There was only one day that anyone else saw true, pure, unbridled Red. Truth be told, I don't remember exactly when it was. At a certain point in the timeline of depression, the months and years start to blur together. It was not a good day, and Mom and I had just arrived back at my apartment. I think we were returning from yet another underwhelming appointment. I was exhausted from fighting my demons, devastated that I couldn't will myself to make any progress, and enraged by the whole situation. If I were a cartoon character, there would have been smoke pouring out of my ears. But I didn't want Mom to see it. I thought it would scare her, and my depression had already hurt her enough. She'd been through hell and back more times than I could count because of me. She sat down on my couch, and I walked back to my bed, blood boiling. I sat down, trying to keep the burning red lava inside of me. I gritted my teeth, dug my fingernails into my legs, and tried to maintain control. I didn't care what other color I ended up at. At whatever cost, I couldn't let Mom see Red.

I had no sense of time. It may have been thirty seconds of me digging my nails into my legs, or maybe it had been thirty minutes when Mom came over. She sat down beside me and could see clear as day that I was on the brink of an eruption. It was like watching the ball drop on New Year's Eve, except Ryan Seacrest isn't involved, and it's counting down to an uncontrollable emotional meltdown rather than a happy celebration and Jenny McCarthy kissing What's His Name Wahlberg. Mom made one mistake—a mistake that she couldn't possibly have known would set me off. She tried to hold my hand. She pried my fingers from my thigh and tried to hold my hand to calm me down. But I was Red, and Red wasn't going to be fixed that easily. I gripped her hand as tightly as I'd been squeezing my leg, but after just a few seconds I realized I was crushing her fingers. I was doing the one thing I so desperately wanted to avoid. I was hurting her.

I lost it. Erupted. I don't know if you've ever seen a twenty-something-year-old throw a full-on temper tantrum, but that was pretty much the scene. Every fiber of my being pulsed with psychotic rage. I wanted to obliterate everything in sight. I wanted to punch holes in the wall, smash every plate, cup and bowl I owned, splinter my bed frame, and rip the limbs clean off my anger management Dammit Doll. Amidst my enraged stupor, I tried to get everything away from me that I might break—unsuccessfully, I might add. I thrashed on the bed, punched everything I could find, and yanked on the headboard of my bed frame, trying to rip it to pieces with my bare hands. I tore a small hole in the seam of my Dammit Doll from ripping her legs apart. I pulled the sheets off my bed and somehow got them all tangled up with each other. Somewhere in the melee, I broke the frames of my glasses.

I don't remember how long it lasted, but I remember screaming over and over that this wasn't fair. I had already gone through this. And I was right. I *had* already gone through this. It was my second depressive episode, which had graduated me to official recurrent major depression status. I had already put my family through the hell of my first episode. I had already punished them with sleepless nights, stressful phone calls, and daily anxiety over my well-being. I had already gone through this. I had already beat this. I had made it through my first episode and had a few years of bliss. I had vowed never to forget how valuable happiness is. I was determined to be a role model for others battling mental illness because I had beat it. I had won.

I think I understand how Peeta and Katniss felt in the second book of the Hunger Games series. The deal was that if you survived and won the Hunger Games, you were removed from the drawing to ever have to go back in—but they got sent back anyway. I felt the same betrayal. I had won. I had beat depression. But it didn't matter; I got sent back in anyway. My name hadn't been removed from the world's worst raffle; it had been added in an extra time.

By the end of the Red eruption, every bone and muscle in my body ached. I don't think it was from the physical thrashing as much as the full-body tension I had sat with beforehand. I lay in my destroyed bed, panting and silently crying. Mom sat on the edge of the bed as I sobbed, and gave me the same back rub she used to give me as a child when I had a nightmare. It wasn't fair. I had already gone through this. I hated my brain for being what it was, hated God for making it that way, hated every doctor for not being able to fix it, and hated myself for the cancerous pain it spread to my loved ones.

Every so often, I still get annoyed about it. Try as I might to avoid it, the simple thought of "why me?" creeps in from time to time. I know depression is a disease I can't control. I know it isn't my fault that I had a first episode or a second. I know I didn't do anything to deserve it. I know I did nothing to cause it, but why did I lose the mental health lottery? Why did I get stuck with the jacked-up brain? Major recurrent depression doesn't run in the family; Mom, Dad, Brianna, my biological grandparents…none of them had the cards I was dealt. Alzheimer's is coming down the pipeline on my Mom's side (Lord help us on that one), but where did this come from? And why me? Why me?

Anytime I start going down the *Why me?* path, I'm reminded of a quote I saw years ago: "If you're going to ask God 'why me?' when bad things happen, you also have to ask, 'why me?' when good things happen." And I get that. I'm sure God gets sick of people constantly asking for things and never coming back to say thank you. If Bruce Almighty was any indication, God has a pretty tough job with a lot of people to balance.

I also know that I could do a lot better in the gratitude department (in my defense, the whole chemically imbalanced brain incapable of producing sufficient happiness does make gratitude a little tricky). But still...could you cut me a break, Big Man Upstairs? I'm just saying, I'll happily trade some of my great moments if we can knock a few years off this depression sentence. I'll give you my Mock Trial State Championship in exchange for wrapping up this episode by the end of the year. And you can have my limited-edition Oregon Pit Crew Jordan 3s if you agree not to give me a third episode. Or all of my gaming consoles and games in exchange for never going to full Red again. So...deal? Maybe? Think about it and let me know. I'll be praying.

Everybody Needs a Kevin

Support systems are everything. Of all the things I wouldn't be here if not for, my support system is number one by a mile. When most people think of support systems, they think about family members and maybe a few close friends. Beyond the standard blood relative support system, my big three supporters were *The Great British Bake Off*, Tater Tot, and Kevin.

The Great British Bake Off

Let's start with the simplest: *The Great British Bake Off* is the best TV show ever made, bar none. It is cheery and heartwarming and just pure, unfettered delight. I want nothing more than to take lessons from the incomparable Paul Hollywood. Every time I bake, I make sure there are no soggy bottoms, so as not to disappoint the legendary Mary Berry. When things don't turn out as cleanly as they should, I simply refer to them as "informal," à la Mary Berry. I yell "Ready, Set, BAAAAKE" along with Mel and Sue in every episode, and incorporate "tutty bye" into my daily life as often as I can. I have Martha's cookbook. I quote Ruby whenever possible. I will go to my grave swearing that Rahul didn't deserve to win (I'm sorry, Rahul, but you really choked there at the end, and I just can't look past that. But you seem like a great guy.).

There are so many seasons of *The Great British Bake Off* on Netflix that it gave me a few solid months of distraction. I wasn't looking for TV shows to make me happy; I just needed something to break the silence of my apartment as I waited for the day to end. *Enter The Great British Bake Off*, which is now my go-to pick-me-up show. Whether they know it or not (in this case, definitely not) Paul, Mary, Prue, Mel, and Sue are my support system. Thanks, guys.

Tater Tot

Support system element number two: Tater Tot. Not the delicious form of potato, but the hamster. At the beginning of my second episode, I had serious doubts about my ability to take care of myself. My hygiene was questionable, eating was sporadic, cleaning was minimal, and I'd only leave the house for work. I was lonely by choice, but Mom and I both thought that having someone or something to take care of might help. If I couldn't fight to get out of bed just for myself, perhaps I could do it for someone who needed me to survive. In late October of 2018, Mom and I headed to PetSmart and bought Tater Tot, my therapy hamster and new best friend. I thought Tot would be an adorable, sweet, mentally stable furball and a nice balance to my wildly unstable existence. Whether by fate, karma, lack of information from PetSmart, or mere coincidence, "sweet, mentally stable furball" wasn't exactly what I got. I didn't get the perfect therapy pet to balance my challenges. I got my twin. In hamster form. Just like me at the time, Tater Tot was a little bonkers. Truly unhinged, if you will.

She was a cutie; I'll give her that. But in hindsight, there were some red flags that maybe we should have paid more attention to in those first couple of hours. Red flag number one was when the PetSmart employee never actually touched Tater Tot; she scooped the hamster into a box and slammed the lid shut. Tater Tot went ballistic in the car for the entire one-mile drive back to my apartment. When we got home and opened the box, red flag number two appeared: Tot had decimated the cardboard, to an extent I've seen only from woodchippers and paper shredders—not from lil' hammies who were in the box for literally less than ten minutes.

The disasters with Tater Tot began the moment she got home. I opened the box to lift her out and put her in the cage, which turned out to be my first critical error. Red flag number three was when she was nice and calm for maybe half a second, then scurried up my shirt to my shoulder and promptly took a flying, peeing leap off, landing hard on the kitchen floor. She then proceeded to sprint around the kitchen, peeing and pooping everywhere she went, as I desperately tried to snag her. Mom kept telling me to make sure Tot didn't go under the fridge or oven, I fruitlessly tried to get a grip of this seven-dollar demonic jumping bean, and then I had a nice little panic attack and started hyperventilating. Mom finally got Tot into the cage, and that is how my journey with Tater Tot began.

I wish I could tell you that things quickly got better, but they most certainly did not. I initially thought I was just an incompetent pet owner, and after about four days I seriously considered accepting defeat and bringing Tot back to PetSmart. I couldn't touch her without her going nuts, and on the off chance that she didn't just bolt and hide, she'd bite my fingers and not let go. She had a little bedroom attic area in her cage that she would regularly fill with so much bedding and poop that it blocked the only entrance, thus cutting off her access to food and water. She ran on top of her wheel instead of in it.

As much as I wanted to get rid of her, though, I couldn't bring myself to do it. I couldn't give up on her. Maybe I was projecting a need for my support system not to give up on me, but for whatever reason, I doubled down on my commitment to Tater Tot and began my extensive hamster research. I got her a new cage better suited for her breed, since it turns out the PetSmart employee had given us wildly inaccurate advice[28]. Her new favorite activity then became climbing up the bars to the top of the cage and then just…letting go. Splatting herself onto the bottom of the cage time and time again. I spent nearly $300 on new toys to keep her life exciting, in the hopes that other activities would discourage the skydiving she was getting hooked on. I bought a playpen and a jungle gym so she could get plenty of exercise.

I also began the arduous process of taming her. I don't know if you've ever tried to tame a hamster, but with Tater Tot it was nothing short of an ordeal. I needed her to get comfortable with me in an environment where she couldn't run away. As I learned from the various hamster discussion boards and forums, an empty bathtub was the best place to do that. Each night I'd coax Tater Tot into her exercise ball, get some fresh veggies to

---

[28] I have some serious beef with PetSmart. Those people are a scam and/or entirely clueless. How do you not sell cages appropriate for the animals you're selling as part of the package deal?

make her happy, climb into the empty bathtub fully clothed, and let Tot loose. The idea was that she just needed to explore me and get used to my smell, but since she was fundamentally a disturbed little menace, the way she achieved that was by nibbling on anything she could latch her sharp little teeth onto. On day two of taming, when I realized that I was going to have some serious battle scars if we continued the same approach, I adjusted my wardrobe. For the next few weeks, I'd get home, put on my thickest jeans, two pairs of socks, a hoodie, and a beanie that covered my ears, and then let Tot loose. She nibbled on so many things, but after eight weeks of nightly taming, we finally had a breakthrough. I could pet her without her cowering in fear, running away and peeing, or otherwise spazzing out.

I was proud of myself, not just for the results of my hard work, but because of how hard I had worked. There weren't many things I had been able to stick to and regularly take care of during my depressive episode—myself included—so having found success with Tot meant everything. I had finally earned a gold star.

The next two weeks were paradise, and I couldn't wait to show Mom everything Tater Tot and I had achieved. We scheduled a dinner on Friday night, when Mom would have the chance to see all of Tater Tot and my progress. I played with Tot a few evenings before Mom's dinner—to make sure we were ready for the big demonstration of her relative sanity—and she chomped my thumb so hard that she managed to punch right through my nail and leave teeth marks on both sides of my thumb. This was not ideal and reminded me that the taming process was not going to be linear; it was a journey just like everything else.

The next day wasn't the best for me emotionally, so Mom came over after work to hang out and make sure I was okay. While she was there, I figured I might as well show her how well Tater Tot and I were doing. As we waited for Tot to wake up (hamsters are nocturnal, and Tot usually got up around 8 p.m.), we got takeout Chinese food from a restaurant around the corner from my apartment. Mom made me walk to the restaurant, largely to require me to get dressed and leave the apartment. We returned with our dinner around 7:45, ate dinner, and finished cleaning up around 8:15. Tater Tot still wasn't up, and she hadn't even rustled or made a single sound.

Mom was ready to head home, and I was losing patience waiting for Tot to wake up and show her much-improved behavior. I stuck my hand in the cage to wake her up and coax her out of bed with a carrot. She didn't immediately look to bite me or hide or pee somewhere absurd. Something wasn't right. I pulled her out of the cage and knew that there absolutely was something wrong. I instantly burst into hysterical tears; I'm talking full-on Hollywood-style knees hugged against my chest, rocking back and forth, sobbing. Tater Tot was alive—she still had a pulse and was breathing on her own—but that was about it.

Mom had talked to a hamster breeder on Craigslist when I was first getting Tater Tot. As I cried over Tater Tot's helpless body and tried to get her to eat or drink water, Mom emailed the Craigslist guy to see if there was anything we could do. The short answer was no, but I refused to accept that answer. I was ready to call 911 for Tater Tot. Mom talked me out of that, but I did convince her to call the only veterinary urgent care in the area that was open. As it turns out, urgent care vet centers are intended more for dogs and cats than hamsters (rude), so they didn't have

140

any small animal specialists on call. If I'd had more energy, I would have been very upset with them. I mean, honestly. How are you going to call yourself an emergency urgent care for animals if you don't have the right team to take care of my animal in an urgent emergency situation? I'm calling shenanigans on their entire operation. False advertising.

But anyway…Mom was simultaneously trying to figure out if there was any hope for Tot and texting Dad to let him know she'd be spending the night at my apartment because we were in complete crisis mode. I contributed nothing to the problem-solving efforts, just sat sobbing and willing Tater Tot to live.

I'll give Tot so much credit; she was an absolute fighter. She showed symptoms of having had a stroke and was having small seizures every few minutes. I cried endlessly as I tried to manually work her back legs while she tried to use her front legs. I put a bottle cap of water in front of her and tried to help her drink water; I refused to believe that it was all over for Tater Tot, especially when we had just had our breakthrough with each other. After enough of my begging, Mom finally conceded that if Tater Tot made it through the night, we could take her to the vet first thing the next morning. Guided only by the delusion that Tater Tot could potentially survive and recover, I agreed, then cried myself to sleep.

By the time we woke up the next morning, Tater Tot had moved on to the big hamster wheel in the sky. Mom let Brianna know that Tater Tot had passed away, to which she had a very simple response: "All that damn hamster had to do was stay alive."

So, you know what sucks? When your pet dies. You know what sucks even more? When it's your therapy pet that was supposed to help you navigate through a second episode of recurrent major depression. You know what sucks *even more*? When you spent twelve weeks getting that little nut to like you and as soon as they do, they croak. And you know what sucks the most? When all that goes down four days before Christmas.

I ended up with quite a random assortment of Christmas gifts that year; most of what Mom and Dad had bought me was for Tater Tot, but it didn't seem like the best move to keep all those under the tree when Tater Tot was buried in the yard. So, I got a toilet seat heater. Honestly, it's pretty rad, and I'd definitely recommend it. Nothing makes you feel classier than taking a seat on a nice warm seat and knowing that it's intentionally warm (as opposed to leftover warmth from a stranger on a public bathroom seat). But I would have traded the toilet seat for more time with Tater Tot in a heartbeat.

Epilogue: After reading the fine print in the PetSmart contract, we found out that if you buy a hamster from them and it doesn't work out, you can return it and they'll sell it again. And again. And again. My theory is that Tater Tot was at least 18 months old when I got her and had been returned multiple times. She was a cranky old lady who had been bounced around various houses and families, and it probably messed her up a little more each time.

It took me a few years to fully recover from Tater Tot and find it in me to get a new hamster. In January 2021, Mom and I took an hour-long road trip to get a new lil' hammy. We weren't going to run any risk of getting another old hamster that only had a few months left of life. We picked up a little guy who was born happy (probably) and healthy just four weeks prior. I named him Dobby, and he is the love of my life. Remember those Christmas presents for Tater Tot that Mom and Dad had yanked out from under the tree? Take a guess what Dobby got for his three-month birthday.

Kevin

Last, but certainly not least, is Kevin. Everybody needs a Kevin. A lot of the names in this book I changed for privacy or because I don't know if I'm allowed to put doctors' or therapists' real names on blast like that, but Kevin gets to keep his name because that's how big of a role he played in my road to recovery. When you look for your Kevin, you're looking for someone who can be an absolute rock through all the ups and downs, will be there at the drop of a hat when you're in crisis, can tell when you're having a bad time without saying anything, and yet treats you no differently despite it all. Written out like that, I realize that finding a Kevin might not actually be that easy. I might just have been incredibly lucky to have had him in my corner.

To backtrack, I met Kevin in high school. He was a freshman when I was a junior, and I thought he was a royal pain. An absolute nuisance. A complete pest. I couldn't stand the twerp. It took about eighteen months for us to slowly become friends, but as I grew to know the heart underneath the pest, I started to understand his character. He was never the type of person to be grand and emotional, but the people who were lucky enough to really know Kevin got to see the unfailing compassion deeply ingrained in him. The night before I left for Oregon—when I already had that gut feeling it was going to be all wrong—he stayed until the last minute and helped pack up the truck. Without saying it, he knew I needed someone to lean on, and he was there for me.

When I dropped out of college, he didn't skip a beat. We never had a deep conversation about what exactly had happened, largely because I didn't want to have that conversation with anyone at all, but he was never more than a phone call away. Whether it was tennis in the park, pickup basketball, trips to Dairy Queen, or rides to and from work, Kevin effortlessly took my mind off whatever was bothering me. I hope I was able to reciprocate that for him sufficiently when his life took its knocks because I don't know if I'll ever be able to find the words to express my gratitude.

The thing with Kevin—and the thing that you need to find in your own Kevin—is how truly effortless his support is. He doesn't need to try to be a rock; he just is. He doesn't have to work at being compassionate; it's his nature. During my first depressive episode, beginning at Oregon and carrying over into being back home, I worked hard not to let anybody see how much I was struggling. Evidently, I was very successful. About a year later, when I finally got tired of lying to everyone outside of my nuclear family, I did what any good millennial would: I wrote a blog post about it. I emailed the link to Kevin, with the idea that it would just sort of fill in any gaps he might have had in understanding what my last year or so had been about.

As it turned out, he genuinely had no clue what I was going through. Being the caring man that he is, he took that incredibly personally. He unnecessarily shouldered guilt for not seeing my pain; we had spent time together nearly every day in that time, and he piled disappointment on himself for not seeing what I was working so hard to hide. He didn't realize that his *not* knowing was precisely what I needed. I needed someone to treat me like a totally normal human. I needed someone to make fun of

144

me and crack jokes about my noodle arms without fearing it would trigger a depressive breakdown. I needed him not to know, and because his inherent compassion was so strong, he was able to be exactly what I needed without knowing it and without me needing to ask for it.

When the second episode began, Kevin was my assistant coach for a high school girls' basketball team. And let me tell you, that team sucked. We were horrible. We lost multiple games by at least fifty points. There were games I wasn't sure we'd ever actually get the ball through the hoop—hell, there were even practices I wasn't confident we'd ever make a shot. The phrase "world's worst group of athletes" may or may not have been thrown around in conversation (unless any of y'all who were on that team are reading this, in which case you were definitely the exception/you were great/you are WNBA bound for sure/you are a once in a generation talent).

The beginning of the season coincided perfectly with me first starting out on Zoloft, and we all know how well that went. Less than a month into the season, I knew I had to tell Kevin what was going on. I had taken a medical leave of absence from working retail at Nike, but I didn't know what the next few months were going to look like or how they might affect my ability to coach. The last thing I wanted was to have to explain months of mental illness an hour before game time because I was losing my marbles from a bad reaction to Zoloft.

The day I planned to tell him, I was nervous—which, unsurprisingly, he noticed instantly. We stepped outside the gym during warm-ups, and I told him the basics: I was in another depressive episode, things were bad, we were trying out medications, side effects could go wild, and I wanted him to know just in case I needed help. He gave the best response I could have hoped for: "Ok." I didn't have to worry about trying to explain why I was shaking the entire bench with uncontrollable leg twitches, why some days I was too exhausted to demonstrate the drills we were running in practice, why other days I needed to stay late to try to burn off excess restless energy, or why sometimes I needed him to take the reins on dealing with parents.

A couple of months later, I received some bad news only minutes before we tipped off a game. I did my best to push through and focus on the game and lied to Kevin when he asked if I was okay early in the first quarter. Everybody needs a person who knows when you're lying. At halftime, he asked what was going on. I told him, and once again he gave the perfect response: "What do you need?"

All I really needed at that time was a distraction, but I could have asked for the moon, and he would have done whatever he could to make it happen. As the season progressed, he helped me find humor and entertainment out of some of the more ridiculous side effects (the deathly putrid farts were particularly weird, and thankfully short-lived).

If you had told me when I met that little pest that he would become a cornerstone to my mental health, I'd have laughed you out of the room. During the bachelorette weekend before his wedding, I got to chat with his now wife and a few other bridesmaids about how lucky we all are to have Kevin. Everybody needs a person they can go to, dump their problems onto, and not scare away. The next Pro Tip is prioritizing finding that person.

Find the person who will listen to your pain without aggrandizing it. Find the person who can balance compassion without it becoming outright pity. Find the person who refuses to walk on eggshells around you. Find the person who knows what you're going through, understands what you're dealing with, and doesn't allow it to change how they think, talk, or act around you. Find the person who can preserve normalcy. If you're lucky, you can find all that in a single person. Now, did Kevin save my life in the same capacity as Greg or my immediate family? Probably not. But was Kevin exactly who I needed when I needed him? Absolutely. And that's why everybody needs a Kevin.

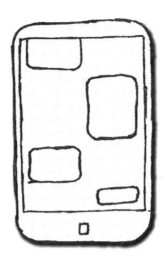

Texting About Feelings

The rapper Logic has a song called "1-800-273-8255". It's about suicide and shares a boy's story from two perspectives (well, kind of three): the boy himself before he calls the National Suicide Prevention Lifeline, the hotline operator who answers the call, and the boy after the call. It is a damn good song and an incredible music video. In fact, let's take another little timeout for five minutes so you can watch it. Either the video or the live performance from the 2017 MTV VMAs. Both are stellar for different reasons. But seriously. Go watch at least one of them. I'll wait.

Are you back? Tissues gone, goosebumps on your arms starting to fade, tears wiped off your face? Cool. Let's continue.

I hate the phone. Hate it, hate it, hate it. If I ever doubt my identity as an introvert, putting a phone in front of me will change that in a heartbeat. If I'm deciding where I want to get dinner, and one restaurant has the option to order online and the other I have to call, the decision is made. Boom, done, settled. I'm ordering online. End of discussion. I don't like delivering any news on the phone, whether good or bad. Please just text me and let me text you back, and don't make me talk on the phone.

So, when the only hotlines available were phone hotlines, it wasn't gonna happen for me. I was a big advocate to other people that they should use hotlines when needed, and it was great that people were there to talk—and overall, just yay for hotlines! But you couldn't pay me to call a hotline, let alone do so when I was already in crisis. Take one of your biggest fears and throw it on top of an emotional breakdown. If you lost a loved one and I told you that there was someone to help you, but they were sitting in a lion's den in the Sahara, you'd probably try to find another way to cope. Not happening.

That's how I felt about calling a hotline. I would rather continue having an emotional breakdown and stay miserable and cry myself to sleep than pick up a phone and call someone who could help me. But I'll send a text. And that's what this mini-chapter is about. The crisis text line that saved my life.

Christmas 2018 was a bad time, to say the least. A really bad time. Tater Tot died on the 21st, and on the 26th I decided I would take my own life. Remember a couple of chapters back when I said the night in Ireland was the second-worst of my life? Here comes number one. Major trigger warning.

Christmas is my favorite time of year, bar none. I fought hard to be cheerful for Christmas day— so hard that I had completely burnt myself out before the end of the day.

After opening presents, I had a breakdown while deciding if I should go to my aunt and uncle's for Christmas dinner. That was it. That was the extent of the decision that needed to be made. It didn't matter what I wore, if we left on time, or how long we stayed. It was completely understandable if I didn't go, and Brianna was happy to stay home to keep me company. Even if we went to dinner as a family and I wasn't feeling it, I could have slept, stayed in the car, or even driven home. All I had to decide was if I was going to hop in the car with Mom and Dad. And it broke me. It absolutely broke me. I ended up on the floor of Brianna's bedroom, once again sobbing hysterically. I didn't want to go, but I didn't want to let down the family—in hindsight, it is crystal clear that not going wouldn't have disappointed anybody, but in the moment, it was all I could think of. I decided to go, to power through the evening even though I was running on fumes —and burning through them at an unsustainable pace.

The next morning, I couldn't do it anymore. I couldn't take another day of the unbearable pain. I went down to San Jose for basketball practice in the morning and decided not to go back home to my parents' house afterward. I knew I didn't want to live anymore, but was hanging on for dear life. I couldn't take the risk of driving home, let alone on the freeway. Every time I thought about ending my life, I thought about how easy it would be to get on an empty freeway, accelerate, point my car at the concrete center divider and let go of the wheel. It would be so easy, so simple, and so fast.

I texted Mom that I was going to stay in San Jose because I didn't want to drive. I could feel myself losing my grip, and I knew that if I got behind the wheel, I would put my car into a wall. Mom and I texted sporadically over the next three hours; she pleaded with me to come home, and I shut down entirely. I couldn't burden her with my pain. I couldn't tell her the thoughts taking control of me. My mind was screaming back and forth, arguing with myself whether to live or die. I thought the safest place for me was locked in my apartment by myself. I thought that with enough time, I could regain control. Hours passed, and nothing improved.

By 6 p.m., after being alone in the apartment for hours on end, my will to fight was running out. I paced back and forth, sobbing, desperately fighting through each minute. In hindsight, it's obvious: I should have called 9-1-1. I lived a block from a firehouse, and three blocks from the police department. As early as preschool, we're taught that if you're in danger or you think someone might try to hurt you, you call 9-1-1. Granted, in preschool, they don't exactly cover the idea that *you* might be the person at risk of hurting you, but the basic sentiment is there: if your safety is at risk, you call 9-1-1. You don't try to fix it yourself, and you don't call a friend or parent and hope they can sort it out. You call 9-1-1 and let the professionals protect you. For the rest of my life, I'll be kicking myself because I should have called 9-1-1. My life was at risk. I was undeniably a danger to myself, and I should have called for help…but I hate the phone.

I texted Mom again, saying that I didn't want to drive because I thought I would crash. She offered to come to pick me up or request an Uber for me. I told her I didn't want any of that, and that I wanted to be done. I told her I didn't want any help and I was sorry, but it was okay. I was ready to be done.

Amidst my loss of self, I vaguely recalled reading about a crisis text line. I don't know what in me drove me to text it, but I did. I'm not a hugely religious person, but I have to believe it was God or some sort of guardian angel who took the wheel and pushed me to text the crisis line. A crisis counselor responded instantly and calmly. She didn't push me for any other information or make it feel like a formal process. She listened (or read, since it was text). She got me to breathe. She got me to articulate what I was feeling and how bad things were. She got me to breathe again. She got me to call Brianna, who stayed on the phone with me while Mom broke every speed limit on her way down to San Jose to pick me up. I couldn't say much on the phone; the physical, mental, and emotional pain had completely taken me over. I sobbed on the phone to Brianna as the text operator continued to check in on me. She kept pulling responses out of me to make sure I was alive until Mom arrived.

Once Mom got there, I broke down into her arms and forgot to reply to the crisis line. The counselor sent a few more texts until I replied, again making sure I was okay. I don't know her name, what she looks like, or anything about her life. I don't know what led her to become a crisis text line counselor, or if she works another job. All I know is that without her and the Crisis Text Line, I would not be sitting here today.

The Crisis Text Line number is **741-741**. Save it for a rainy day.

Intermission #2

The "Frozen" Franchise Is Actually About the Stigma of Mental Health and the Process of Recovery

Yes, I know these are the second and third children's movies I've recommended, but they are objectively fantastic, so get off your high horse and go watch them. This also escalated into a very long intermission and is jam-packed with spoilers, so if you haven't yet seen *Frozen* and *Frozen II*, stick a bookmark on this page and go marathon them really quick.

All done? Excellent. Enjoy having "Let it Go" stuck in your head for the next 8–10 business days. You're welcome.

Let's start by unpacking our characters. Number one: Elsa (blondie, blue dress, magic hands, loads of issues). From a very young age, Elsa is different from the rest of the world. The other people in her community can't see it, and she's battling something she can't always control but is trying to make the best of. Her parents are out of their depth because she has challenges they've never faced. They see Elsa's differences as something to be ashamed of, or something to hide, which leads Elsa to feel the same way. They are confused, Elsa is confused, and Elsa's sister Anna is confused. They talk to a specialist (the troll) who gives them some guidance, but he really isn't *that* directly helpful. Sound familiar? In case you haven't picked up what I'm putting down...news flash, y'all: Elsa's experience with her uncontrollable icy spears is pretty darn similar to most people's experience with mental illness.

I, a person with chronic mental illness, am different from the rest of the world, and while others can't see it, I'm trying to control and make the best of it. My family is out of their depth because they've never before had a child with mental illness. It's something I'm inexplicably ashamed of, and most of the specialists we talk to are sort of helpful but in an awfully indirect approach.

Character number two: Anna. In almost every situation with a pair of sisters, I bear a striking resemblance to the younger sister and Brianna is a dead ringer for the older. She's Beezus, I'm Ramona. She's Susan, I'm Lucy. She's Katniss, I'm Prim. *Frozen* is one of the few examples that it gets flipped. I'm Elsa. I'm the messed up one. She's pure-of-heart Anna, who just wants to be there for her sister but doesn't always know how and can't fully understand what Elsa is going through. Granted, Anna's approach is a little more my style (banging on the door and pestering Brianna to play with me until she caves).

Nonetheless, Anna's character is just as important as Elsa's when discussing mental illness. It doesn't just affect the person struggling, and as we find out later in the film, part of Elsa's fear and guilt was because she had hurt Anna with her powers. It's one thing to be struggling internally, but when your once-personal struggles begin to impact and hurt the people you love most, there is a definite shift. To your loved ones, though, it can seem as though you're shutting them out for no reason. That confusion on the part of the loving family member is beautifully articulated in "Do You Want to Build a Snowman?"[29]: *They say, "have courage" and I'm trying to. / I'm right out here for you, just let me in.*

Anna is on one side of a locked door, with Elsa on the other. After Anna delivers her last few lyrics, the camera pans out, and you see a heartbroken Elsa surrounded by a clearly uncontrolled eruption of her powers. She desperately wants to let Anna into the room, and proverbially "in" to her struggles, but is so terrified to hurt Anna again that it seems safer to shut her out entirely.

And then we have the single greatest animated musical number in the history of mankind[30]: "Let it Go."[31] Aside from the stunning videography, the song shows a unique but critical moment within mental illness: the freedom and relief that comes from giving up. Giving up the charade, giving up the shame, and

---

[29] Anderson-Lopez, Kristen and Lopez, Robert. Lyrics to "Do You Want to Build a Snowman?" Performed by Kristen Bell, Agatha Lee Monn and Katie Lopez, Wonderland Music Company, 2013. AZLyrics. https://www.azlyrics.com/lyrics/kristenbell/doyouwanttobuildasnowman.html

[30] I will accept arguments that "Let it Go" should fall second, but only to "Circle of Life". Maybe tied with "I'll Make a Man Out Of You," but the Mulan soundtrack hasn't aged super well, so I think that holds it in third place.

[31] Anderson-Lopez, Kristen and Lopez, Robert. Lyrics to "Do You Want to Build a Snowman?" Performed by Idina Menzel, Wonderland Music Company, 2013. AZLyrics. https://www.azlyrics.com/lyrics/idinamenzel/letitgo.html

giving up the feeble attempts to hide what has been pulsing through you. In the first verse, Elsa claims her stage:

A kingdom of isolation, and it looks like I'm the queen
The wind is howling like this swirling storm inside
Couldn't keep it in, heaven knows I've tried

Then we hit the breakthrough. This song is Elsa's celebration. She can't change the hand she's been dealt (her hands literally shoot out ice, and my brain doesn't make enough serotonin…pretty much samesies). Elsa isn't a victim of her circumstances anymore—she's the Queen of them. She is in control. She is their ruler. It's still a kingdom of isolation, which certainly isn't ideal, and she's still got howling wind and a swirling storm, which also aren't ideal, but at least it's hers. It's her kingdom, and she's owning it. She has some extent of control over the kingdom.

Psychologist Kristen Neff presents the "suffering equation," as one of my many therapists explained to me[32]. The equation itself is simple: Pain x Resistance = Suffering. We all experience pain. It's inevitable. No matter how good of a life you live, there's always a chance you'll stub your toe. Or spill your coffee. Or get rear-ended. Or lose a loved one. Or any other small pain or inconvenience that happens every single day. Pain on its own isn't that bad. It's the multiplier—the resistance—that can spiral out of control. When you fight against the pain, whether by burying it, ignoring it, distracting from it, or obsessing over it, that's when you create suffering.

---

[32] Neff, K. (2013). *Self-Compassion*. Hodder & Stoughton.

If you break your arm, it's going to hurt. The broken arm is the finite pain, and your response to it determines your level of suffering. If you try to keep playing basketball with your broken arm, it will continue to hurt; it may even get worse. You'll create more suffering than the original break would have caused. If you see a doctor, put it in a cast, and let it rest for however many weeks is recommended, you're far less likely to have to suffer as much.

The idea of creating resistance—and in turn, magnifying pain—is something I've had a lot of trouble with, especially when it comes to depression. Whenever I have a bad day (pain), I have a few choices. I could push through it and pretend to be totally fine. I could get frustrated with myself for having a bad day. I could get angry with God and the universe for giving me a brain that was insufficiently quality-checked before getting shipped out. But all of those are different kinds of resistance. All of those prolong or create more suffering for me. There is always the choice to take it easy on myself; allow myself to have a crummy day and give it time to heal and recover. The pain is inevitable, but the suffering can be lessened.

In "Let It Go," Elsa has figured that out. She cannot change her pain, but she can stop resisting it. I mean, she stops resisting so much that she literally builds a castle out of her pain, and that's honestly impressive. Jumping on down to the second verse and bridge, Elsa's celebration grows even more:

> ...*The fears that once controlled me can't get to me at all.*
> *My power flurries through the air into the ground.*
> *My soul is spiraling in frozen fractals all around.*
> *And one thought crystallizes like an icy blast,*

I'm never going back, the past is in the past.

She no longer feels the need to conceal what she's going through. She's no longer afraid of herself. She's embracing her power. She's embracing her soul and who she truly is. She's embracing the present and vowing never to go back to that place of darkness and shame (best of luck with that, Elsa). The lyrics that end the song truly capture the moment of relief: "Let the storm rage on. / The cold never bothered me anyway." She can't change the storm. She can't contain the storm by wearing gloves. She can't cure her mental illness. But by God, she can let the storm rage on, dance in the rain, and build a snowman.

The moment Elsa finds a way to shed the stigma, she finally feels free. Again, critical detail that she isn't "cured." She's still the same person she was in Arendelle, but at least she now feels free to authentically be that person. That's delightful, but digging a little deeper reveals the true cost of the mental health stigma. Her parents were so ashamed and afraid of what she was going through that the only people they could go to for help were a literal colony of trolls. Elsa thought she was the only one dealing with those issues—and in *Frozen*, she pretty much was.

In *Frozen II*, though…it turns out she's not the only one! She was just kept separate from the others who experienced similar challenges. She never had a dialogue with the others or had the opportunity to lean on them for support. Not a single person spoke about their powers, which left Elsa feeling entirely alone. For God's sake, she had to leave town and build herself a new castle all by herself before she was able to feel that freedom. That is an excessive response—arguably the single most excessive possible approach to escape the stigma. Most of us don't have the liquid assets to pick up and move to the middle of nowhere and build a castle and start our own stigma-free world. Most of us are relatively stuck where we are; we can't flee to find relief and freedom.

So, let's talk about *Frozen II*. For starters, it has to be one of the most beautifully shot animated movies I've ever seen. Between the water horses and the colored leaves…wow. Just wow. Well done, Pixar animators. *Frozen* focused a lot on Elsa, with her "powers" acting as the metaphor for mental illness. She's born with them, and there appears to be no trigger. *Frozen II* turns the mental health lens on Anna. Anna is devastated when Elsa goes missing and is presumed to be dead (I know…quite dark for a kids' movie). It's an undeniably triggering event, and yet, though the trigger makes sense, Anna isn't convinced that her response is right. The number of times I've heard people with mental illness try to separate what they're feeling from a more common feeling using the phrase "but not like this" is astounding. I've used it countless times myself; I've felt sad, but not like this. I've felt nervous, but not like this. And there it is in the first line of Anna's emotional exploration song, "The Next Right Thing":

> *I've seen dark before, but not like this*
> *This is cold, this is empty, this is numb*
> *The life I knew is over, the lights are out*
> *Hello, darkness, I'm ready to succumb.*

Frozen II really didn't pull any punches. They went right for the heart, and they did not miss. What Anna feels isn't a regular old "sad." It's world-changing, gut-wrenching darkness. She doesn't have the words for the feeling; she just feels the darkness and has no will to fight it:

This grief has a gravity, it pulls me down
But a tiny voice whispers in my mind
You are lost, hope is gone

"This grief has a gravity" is a terrific lyric. My heart goes out to whoever wrote it because I don't think you can capture that sentiment so beautifully and so accurately without having experienced it. When you lose someone that you love, the world feels heavy. Gravity feels stronger. Not only are you down in the dumps emotionally, but it truly seems like you are physically being pulled down as well.

And then there's that damn little voice. Jiminy Cricket's evil cousin or something. It isn't a devil on your shoulder; it's more like a void on your shoulder. It isn't telling you to do anything bad or harmful; it's telling you that there's nothing you can do to fix yourself or the current situation. But then we get to the next line, the hook of the song:

But you must go on
And do the next right thing.
Take a step, step again.
It is all that I can to do
The next right thing
I won't look too far ahead
It's too much for me to take.

Later on, I'll talk a bit about how I can't stand the sentiment of "take things one day at a time!" when you're up to your neck in depressive symptoms. The next right thing, though, is manageable. It's one thing. It's getting out of bed. It's having something to eat. It's feeding your pet. It's getting on a bus to the movies. It's sitting in the rain. I may not be able to face a week, a day, or even an hour. I can't face those concrete benchmarks and count on having the capacity to reach a certain set of goalposts. The idea of the next thing is abstract. It isn't a specific amount of time I have to reach, only for the goalposts to move when I arrive. As Anna sings, "But break it down to this next breath, this next step / This next choice is one that I can make."

One breath. Now that is something I can manage. I can do that. I can take one breath. One choice: pants or shorts? Cereal or pop tarts? Lie on the floor or lie on the couch? *The Great British Bake Off* or *Dancing with the Stars*? I can make one choice, as long as I don't look beyond it. I can do the next right thing. In Anna's case, she's able to "next right thing" her way to the movie's happy ending. Eventually, I'll get to my equivalent of fade to black, roll the credits, and play happy songs; but for now, I'll settle for making it through each breath, each choice, and each moment.

I Could Always Just...Die

To me, Brianna has one of the most stressful lifestyles imaginable. She isn't just a twelfth-hour kind of person... she's a thirteenth-hour kind of person. She once showed up at immigration in an airport in Chile without the requisite paperwork. Unlike most humans who would have been kindly kicked in the derrière and sent back to the States...she got in. (For what it's worth, she did have the requisite paperwork, it was just in her inaccessible checked luggage). She's the kind of person who has a loose idea of Plan A, a vague concept of what might need to happen if "Plan" A falls through, and an infinite amount of faith that anything after that will ultimately work out.

I, on the other hand, am not that kind of person. I have a Plan A, A 1.1, A 1.2, A 1.3, A 2, B, C...and lord knows how long that list goes. It depends on how big of a decision I'm making, how much anxiety is kicking in, and how tired I am. Deciding on what to have for dinner doesn't usually go past C, choosing which Nike shoes to buy limits itself to the middle of the alphabet, and planning a workout might start dancing towards those end-of-the-alphabet letters that are only good for big points in scrabble…but anything beyond that could require me to dip into the Greek alphabet to cover all of my bases.

Being depressed has a funny way of messing with every single plan you've ever made. On some of the tougher days, I might have a reasonably solid Plan A with very few other versions —partially because I couldn't bring myself to come up with more than one plan, and partially because I couldn't count on even having the energy to make it out of bed and kick Plan A into motion. In the darkest depths, Plan A doesn't even exist. I can't bring myself to make any sort of plan or set a single intention for the day, because I'd much prefer if the day just didn't happen at all.

I first began to understand that my brain was deeply—in some ways, irreparably—imbalanced when I realized that I had a permanent backup plan if all else failed: I could always just…die. Trains come rolling by at all hours of the day, there are plenty of concrete barriers on the freeway, and high buildings and bridges are all over the Bay Area. I found a distorted comfort in knowing that there was, in fact, a kill switch if needed (pun not intended but also kind of unavoidable).

Those thoughts have come to act as something of a benchmark for when things are starting to decline. When I start looking at BART stations a little differently, I know things are getting sketchy. When I look for reasons to walk instead of drive or skip a road trip altogether, I know it's time to double-check I'm taking the right meds, consider if anything in life might be throwing me off, figure out if I'm stressing about something coming up, or if there might be some other explanation. It's also the time I know I should turn to my support system, but if I'm being totally honest, I don't usually start with that. As much as I've sung their praises over the last however many pages, it always takes a little bit of a leap of faith to reach out. Asking for help never gets easier, no matter how many times it proves to be the right decision.

But if I am taking my meds, there's no other stressor, and I can't or don't reach out to my support system, there's always the back burner plan. I could always just die. I could be gone. Every time I read about someone stepping in front of a train, jumping from a height, intentionally overdosing, self-harming, or otherwise taking their own life, it reminds me that it always exists as an option. In a perfect world, I would want to die a hero's death. I work with kids year-round, and I've always known that if the time came, I would put myself in front of a bullet to protect them. Part of that is because children are the most sacred, precious investment we have as a society. But another part is that it would be the easiest way to leave this planet without being the cause of anyone else's pain.

No matter how I die, I like to think that people will be sad. I like to think people will miss me. I also think that when you die, or more specifically, how you die, changes how people remember you. If I die by suicide, I would likely be remembered as someone who had immense struggles that they couldn't overcome. If I die by taking a bullet for a child in a school shooting, pushing an old lady out of the path of a runaway bus, or jumping down into a stampede to protect Simba, it doesn't matter as much what struggles I had. I'm a hero. I am someone who sacrificed myself. In my eyes, that was the best possible solution. See, the thing about suicide that I think many people misunderstand is the goal.

The goal isn't to kill yourself. The goal isn't to be dead. The goal is simply to not have to live your life anymore. It isn't a romanticized vision of emotional devastation; it's a hell of a lot simpler than that. It's a desperation to not have to face the next day of life because there are zero reasons to believe that the next day will be any better than the last. If I die a hero's death, I achieve my goal of not having to face another day, but I also spare my family the embarrassment of having a child who committed suicide. Nobody would ever have to know that deep down, I was ready to be done with this life. But that's all a back burner plan, only should the need arise.

The "back burner" concept of suicide is a weird one. It's a large part of why I struggle to answer doctors' questions honestly. I don't like how they're phrased; it's a little too black and white. *Have you been having thoughts about killing yourself?* If we're being technical, then the answer is yes. But I gotta say, having just two checkboxes seems insufficient for such a complex question. This isn't an elementary school "I like you, do you like me?" situation. To someone who hasn't experienced it, suicidal ideation can appear to be very polar: either you have thought about taking your own life, or you have not.

That being said, if I answer the question honestly and say yes, I'm ringing a bell that is incredibly hard to un-ring. Depending on the doctor, it could turn into anything from them asking some follow-up questions (A+ doctor!), bringing in some sort of mental health professional for me to talk to (B/C doctor), sending me straight to mental health urgent care (D doctor) or jumping straight to a 5150 involuntary hold (F doctor). If it's a decent list of questions, the next one on the list will ask about making specific plans or any immediacy. To be honest, that's usually what I use to determine how truthfully my answer will be. If it's a blanket yes or no, I have to go with no—there isn't usually enough space to fully articulate this whole "back burner kinda sorta plan but not really; it's just like a twisted security blanket" concept. If there is space—either physical space on the paper for me to write things out or emotional space in that I trust the doctor enough to feel confident they won't panic—the likelihood of complete transparency skyrockets.

T he Cummings Graduate Institute for Behavioral Health Studies details suicide as a three-step process; knowing the differences can be crucial in determining the most effective intervention strategies[33]. The first is ideation, where you start thinking about suicide, but the cons still outweigh the pros. The fears outweigh the attractions. The nays outweigh the yays. The darkness is creeping in, but you're not at any immediate risk. Then, there's stage two: planning. Anytime you get asked about suicidal thoughts, if you say you've had the thoughts, the second question is about planning. I used to think that was odd; why would the doctor care if I had a plan? Would they incorporate that information into a treatment plan? *Sinéad needs to take these meds, see this therapist, and cannot be left unattended by trains.* Seemed odd.

Turns out, that's the critical difference between stages one and two. If you have a plan, you are at a significantly higher risk of going through with it. It's no longer a thought bouncing around aimlessly; it has an aim, and you're only one decision away from it

---

[33] Prevent suicide by recognizing early warning signs. Cummings Institute. (2020, November 10). Retrieved October 8, 2021, from https://cgi.edu/biodyne-model-therapists-masters-suicide-assessment-prevention/.

happening. Stage two gets awfully lonely, as the making of plans isn't exactly a collaborative activity. The darkness of stage two can be part of what makes stage three so jarring.

Three is the last stage. In stage one, you think a vacation might be fun. In stage two, you're booking flights. Stage three is takeoff, and there's an inexplicable sort of peace that comes with it. So often, a person battling mental illness will appear to improve in stage three. They aren't wrestling with a decision anymore; the decision has been made. The Cummings Institute suggests that the person's suicide attempt is likely to occur within forty-eight hours of entering stage three.

I don't know where my back-burner suicidal thoughts fall in Cummings' progressive stages. I guess it's stage ½? I am aware of suicide as a theoretical option, but haven't even begun to really think about it. But it is always there. It is always in the back of my mind. Bad day at work? I could always just die. Stress piling up? I could always just die. Feeling sick? I could always just die. Overwhelmed and overworked? I could always just die. Depression coming in with a vengeance and absolutely destroying me? I could always just…die.

"What Could I Have Said?"

I had a hard time finding resources and information about what I was likely to experience with the medications and whatnot, but it's arguably even harder to find information about what to do as a family member or friend of someone battling mental illness. A couple of years ago, when I was solidly past my first depressive episode and in a beautiful state of recovery, Brianna asked me what she could have said or done to help me when things got dark. At the time, I didn't have much of an answer, and truthfully, I'm not sure I have any more of an answer now, but I'm going to give it my best shot.

I wish there was a way that you could feel the enveloping darkness that comes with depression, but only for a split second. I would never indefinitely wish these feelings upon even my worst enemy, but for the sake of understanding, I wish I could fully capture what it feels like. Because before you can say the "right" thing in any situation, you have to understand the situation.

Imagine being told to run a few miles in a thunderstorm, but on the condition that you have to stay completely bone dry. Not a drop of water on any part of your being. You can take an umbrella and wear all the waterproof clothes you own, but you can't get any water on any part of you—clothes and shoes included. When you come back in from the storm, you have to be as dry as the Sahara. Not going to happen, right? Try as you might to avoid it, you are going to get wet. It is inevitable. It is beyond your control. Between puddles, cars splashing, gaps of coverage with your clothes, the wind pushing the rain in a hundred different directions, and everything else, staying dry isn't a logistically feasible option. Really, the only way you could possibly stay completely dry is if it stopped raining. But you're not Mother Nature. You can't stop the rain. That's kind of how it feels to try to save face when you're dealing with depression or any mental illness. It's something of an expectation to be happy, but because of the nature of the beast, that isn't always much of an option. You will get sad, and you can't control that. Just as you will get wet if you run in a thunderstorm, and you can't control that. You can't stop your depression any easier than you can stop the rain.

So, what is the right thing to say? On the one hand, there is no "right" set of words. There is no magical sentence. Nothing you say will stop the rain, just like nothing I do will stop the rain. However, that isn't to say that your words aren't still incredibly valuable. You can't fix me, but you absolutely can give me comfort and support as I trudge through the storm. I'm sure that the most helpful statements vary from crazy to crazy, but here are some of the things that helped me tremendously:

"We're going for a walk."

Fresh air might not technically be a medication, but I can't recall a single day that wasn't at least marginally improved by putting on clothes and going outside. It could be a walk around the block or miles off on a trail. It could be filled with conversation or completely silent. Getting me out of the house, on my feet, and moving in some direction was always a plus.

"Have you showered today?"

If you have to ask, the answer is probably no. It's probably been a "no" for the last few days. Again, showering may not be medicinal, but unless you're the Wicked Witch of the West, it likely can't hurt. Two birds, one stone: eliminating some stench and getting a fresh start. Even if you cry in the shower, it blends in with the water coming out of the shower head, and it's not so bad.

"I love you."

In the words of Blair Waldorf: "Three words. Eight letters. Say it and I'm yours." Okay, so maybe Blair is a little more romantic than this needs to be, but the beginning sentiment is all that matters. It's only three little words, but it's something you can never hear too often. I hated myself every day I was depressed, largely because I knew my pain was hurting my loved ones. A bit of osmosis sadness, if you will. Along with my self-loathing, I was also convinced that deep down, those same loved ones hated me as well. I thought they were angry with me for having a second episode, disappointed with how many days I'd ruined or plans I'd canceled because I was having a particularly bad day, and annoyed with having to accompany me once again on the roller coaster of misery. I assumed they didn't love me. I assumed they couldn't love me. I certainly didn't believe them every time they said they loved me, but it never hurt to hear.

"I'll pick you up for your next appointment."

Mom had to outright bribe me to go to the first appointment with my general practitioner. She picked me up, drove me to the appointment, marched me into the office, waited outside as I talked to the doctor, came with me to talk with the case manager, stuck around to talk to the mental health specialist, and then took me out to breakfast. We went to Marie Callender's. It was horrible. Absolutely awful. Straight dookie. The muffins somehow managed to be simultaneously dry and soggy, the eggs were both overcooked and undercooked, the decor was horrendous, service was slow, portion sizes were massive, and they were out of every good flavor of pie. But it was perfect. Everything about it was so bad that we laughed our way through the entire meal. I hadn't laughed that authentically in weeks, and it felt so, so good.

I had a follow-up appointment two weeks later, and I was nervous about it. I didn't know how I would feel on the day, if I would remember how to get there, if I would get to the door and bail, or if I'd be too much of a mess to drive home afterward. The night before the follow-up, Mom sent me a quick text: "I'll pick you up at 11 tomorrow for the appointment. We can get lunch afterward."

Mom continued to pick me up for every appointment for months. She'd reschedule meetings, eat breakfast or lunch at oddball hours, and make any sacrifice needed to be there for each appointment. Somewhere along the way, I started to almost look forward to the next appointment. 1% because I could get some sort of update on how screwy my head was, 24% because I got to choose whatever food I wanted to get afterward, and 75% because I enjoyed spending time with Mom. Actions really do speak louder than words, and having her there to back me up meant everything.

"You are sick, and losing hope is part of the disease."
Amidst all the chaos going on inside a depressed brain, it is darn near impossible to separate the symptoms you feel from who you truly are as a person. Hopelessness is a real nuisance because of the fundamentally convoluted state it puts you in; you need a little bit of hope to get the energy to remember that your hopelessness is part of the thing you're hoping to get past. Hopefully that made sense. Apologies if it didn't. Separating symptoms from character can get really muddled. Reminding me that even one symptom isn't a part of who I am can be a game-changer.

"This isn't your fault."
It can be unbelievably difficult not to feel at personal fault for causing pain. As a concept, and thinking purely logically, I know it's not my fault. I know I didn't choose it, and I know I didn't do anything to cause it. But in my heart of hearts, it is tough to truly believe. It's kind of like when you're watching a scary movie, and as much as you tell yourself that it's all CGI, it's not real, it's just a movie, blah blah blah…your heart still pounds a little bit, and you still sprint from the kitchen to your bed as soon as you turn out the lights. You can look at the facts from a completely objective perspective and follow the reasoning to a T, but at the end of the

day, you just can't wholeheartedly get on board with it. Again, reinforcing the positives and taking steps to undo the guilt I'm piling on myself can be a massive help.

"I made you a fruit plate."
This one is probably more just for me, but growing up, fruit plates were kind of the go-to when mom made lunch for Brianna and me. It usually involved a banana, a plum, maybe some apples, and perhaps an orange. I realize most people's comfort foods are more like baked goods or family recipes or something, but mine is a nice little fruit plate. It's nothing fancy. Chopped up fruit on a plate. No edible arrangements business or elaborate display. Fruit on a plate. And I love it.

"Let's see a movie/play a board game/literally anything else."
Depression is incredibly lonely. You've got your brain telling you that you're hurting the ones you love and that they'd be better off without you. You've got a complete lack of social energy, and you've got very limited motivation to do anything. Making plans with friends takes a lot of work, and the odds of following through are slim. If you make plans for us, though, and all I need to do is put on clothes and let you pick me up, it might just work out. I always knew Mom loved me, but when she picked up the PS4 controller and attempted to play FIFA with me, that was a whole new level of support. She, Dad, and I would watch TV together most evenings, and they often put up with whatever I wanted to watch—usually *The Great British Bake Off*. If there was a movie we both wanted to see, Mom would take me to the theater. All I had to do was show up.

Most of the time, going to the movies was a great distraction. A few hours completely enveloped in someone else's life and someone else's world provided great relief. Even if the movie was garbage (lookin' at you, *Crimes of Grindelwald*), it was a few hours that my focus was on something other than myself. The only one I regretted watching was *A Star is Born*, but I'm gonna put most of the blame on Mom for that one. To be honest, watching that movie when we did might have been one of the biggest mistakes Mom and I made throughout all of my depressive days. I like Lady Gaga. I like Bradley Cooper. I like movies with songs. The film was getting great reviews and a ton of buzz, so it seemed like a great way to spend an afternoon. I hadn't seen any of the previous versions, but Mom apparently had.

Perhaps she was asleep when she watched it, perhaps she left in the middle, or perhaps she went full Dory for an hour or so and developed some major memory loss. That, or she has truly awful judgment on what movies clinically depressed folks should be watching. The first hour or so was great. Lady Gaga's career was on the rise, Bradley Cooper seemed to be doing alright, the acting was great, and the songs were lovely. Then you hit that last half hour or so when (spoiler alert) everything hits the fan. Everything crumbles, everything falls apart, everything derails, and then Bradley Cooper hangs himself. It's an incredibly accurate portrayal in the sense that no one in his character's world saw it coming—even as an audience member, you don't really piece it together until he gets the rope out—but good God, that was not something a clinically depressed suicidal person needed to or should have been watching. Mom and I also ended up sitting in the front row of the theater, which never makes for a great viewing angle. But if I had to divvy up the blame, I'll say 10% of why it was a terrible movie experience was the crick in my neck, and 90% the suicide plot point that probably wasn't the greatest timing for me. To sum up my thoughts on *A Star is Born*: "Shallow" is a beautiful song. "Always Remember Us This Way" is criminally underrated. Gaga and Bradley are phenomenal actors with incredible chemistry. And I will never ever ever ever never watch that movie again for as long as I live.

If I could go back and tell my loved ones two things, it would be these:

There is no perfectly "right" thing you can say to take away someone else's pain.

Every mentally ill person has a busted brain, to varying extents. Every crazy person is differently crazy. Even from one episode to the next, the crazy changes. Things that helped me in my first episode were useless or made things worse in my second. Things that helped in my second episode never crossed my mind in the first. Hell, things that worked at the beginning of a week may not work anymore just by the end of the same week. But fundamentally, the best things I can suggest for you to say are heartfelt, true statements of love. Tell me you don't know what to say but that you're here for me. I don't expect you to know what to say; hell, I don't even know what to say. But as long as you say it with love, whatever you say will be the right thing.

Even if you do find the right words for the moment, there's a very good chance you'll get some pushback anyway.

Once you've found the right words and said them with all the love in your heart, I still can't guarantee they'll be received perfectly. I might ignore what you've shared. I might push back against what you're saying. I might flat out not believe what you're saying. But, on behalf of the crazies, I ask that you keep saying it. Piece by piece, your words do sink in, and for all you know, those words may end up being the one small flicker we hold on to when the day starts to feel impossibly dark.

On the flip side…here are some of the things that made me want to smack the speaker straight across the face:

Have you tried doing things that make you happy?
I've already ranted about this one enough. But, just to reiterate, if curing depression was as simple as doing fun things, mini-golf courses would be a *much* bigger deal, bowling alleys and arcades would be jam-packed in areas hit hard by seasonal affective disorder, and everything fun in life would cost triple because capitalism likes to profit off of joy.

I'm sure you'll be fine. .
I'm glad you're sure of that because I am sure as hell not. Mostly because of that hopelessness thing. You may think you're being comforting by trying to downplay my pain, but all I'm hearing is that you don't want to deal with my scrambled egg brain and that you want to end the conversation.

It's not that big of a deal.
To you, sure. But the things going on in my head destroy me every day and completely distort my perception of life, and that's kind

of a big deal on my end. If it weren't that big of a deal, I probably wouldn't be telling you about it and looking for support.

Take it one day at a time.

I will admit, for others this may be more helpful. For me, though, it was one of the worst. I have no interest in fighting through Tuesday, only to be met with an equally miserable Wednesday. And then a comparably awful Thursday. And then the doom of Friday. Then an entire weekend with nothing to do while everyone else has great things to do, so I don't want to burden them. I can't count the number of days I opened my eyes, realized it was the start of another day, and completely broke down. Sometimes I'd cry. Sometimes I'd scream into my pillow. Sometimes I'd hold so tightly to the bed frame that my knuckles turned white and my hands went numb. Sometimes I'd punch my mattress. Sometimes I'd go ballistic on my Dammit Doll. Mornings were awful because there was so much time in the day I had to push through. So, thanks but no thanks. I appreciate the sentiment, but I'd rather take it no days at a time if that's an option.

Any variation of "it could be worse/others have it worse."

They absolutely do. I have a roof over my head, clothes on my back, food in the fridge, and a paying job. That puts me ahead of most of the world population. But pain is pain, and mental illness doesn't discriminate based on how good the rest of your life is. I already feel a tremendous amount of guilt for the pain I am putting into my world. Piling on the fact that others have it worse and I don't have the right to feel like I do just makes it worse.

You don't act depressed.

Thanks? To be honest, I could never figure out if this one was a compliment or a cop-out. Am I really good at covering it up? If so, that's almost a compliment—or at least it's a compliment to those of us working hard to hide what we're going through. Or am I simply not "appearing tearful" enough to prove that I'm depressed? Do I need to have more public crying breakdowns rather than contain them in the privacy of my apartment? Are you suggesting that I'm being dramatic when I describe my feelings because they don't match how I act? It's an oddly backhanded compliment, and I never know how to react: concede that I appear to be totally fine and then try to convince you I'm not fine; or start highlighting times when I was "acting depressed" that you may not have noticed. Neither response, nor any parts of the conversation that follow, will make me feel much better.

You just need to eat healthier/sleep more/drink water/meditate/ think positive thoughts/etc.

Not to toot my own horn, but my body is pretty much in tip-top shape. I love berries, drink a gallon of water every day, never get less than eight hours of sleep, exercise regularly, and I even tried to meditate a couple of times. The most alcohol I have is from communion at church, and the only drugs coursing through my veins are my carefully selected antidepressants. For God's sake, I'm a health and PE teacher. Fitness and wellness and health are my whole life. But no matter how many salads I ate or pints of Ben and Jerry's I didn't eat, I was still depressed. Went to the gym…still depressed. Bought whole wheat pasta instead of frozen lasagna…still depressed. Drank fresh fruit protein smoothies for breakfast instead of eating toaster pastries…still depressed. Does having the rest of my life in order increase my likelihood of success? Probably. But will eating only kale, chicken breasts, and brown rice for two months straight cure my chemically imbalanced brain? I'm gonna go with a resounding "probably not."

It's all in your head.
Ding ding ding! Yes, it is all in my head. You are absolutely right. I am aware that crying on Brianna's floor over going to Christmas dinner is something only happening in my screwy brain. I know that not being able to get out of bed—or getting out of bed only to lay on the floor for another few hours—is an issue with my brain. I have fully grasped that the life I'm living and the world I'm experiencing is pretty far off from what others are working with. I understand that my brain is not functioning how it's supposed to and that all of the pain and hopelessness and fatigue and everything else in DSM-5 is in my head. That said, you sharing that observation with me is zero percent helpful. I know I'm bonkers, and I don't really need reminding.

Above all, the biggest thing I can ask on behalf of my fellow crazies is that you stick with us as long as it is healthy for you. It is hard to lie to friends, put on a brave face for loved ones, and force a smile for everyone we see. There will be times we crumble and perhaps even try to push people away. We may try to push you away in an act of self-preservation or to protect you from what we see as a cancerous situation. But please stick around. Just be there. You don't need to say a word. Just be there. You don't have to fully understand what we're going through. Just be there. Send a text, write a letter—anything at all. Just be there.

To the Crazies

I've spent the last however many thousand words speaking my truth on behalf of the crazies who felt the same. This chapter, though, isn't on behalf of the crazies. It's for the crazies.

To my fellow crazies,

Hi there. If you feel like a bit of a nutter in a world of "normals," then we are in the same boat in the same ocean. I know that the whole idea of "normal" is a bunch of baloney in and of itself, but on the spectrum of normalcy, I still feel pretty far off to the crazy side. But more and more, I'm trying to become okay with that. I'm a little bonkers, and that's okay. My brain doesn't work like it's supposed to, and that's okay. I need a little extra help from time to time, and that's okay. All of that applies to you as well. You may be a little bonkers with a slightly malfunctioning brain that needs some extra TLC, and that's okay. In fact, it's more than okay.

Personally, I think it's great. We ought to start a club of all the folks who have to remind ourselves that our quirks are okay.

There's a quote I heard years ago, and it has stuck with me ever since. It's from Iyanla Vanzant, an inspirational speaker, and it reads: "When you tell your story, you free yourself and give other people permission to acknowledge their own story." I started writing this book out of frustration; I couldn't find the answers I was looking for or the dialogue I wanted. I knew that there were millions of people who had made it through what I was facing, tried the medications I was about to be prescribed, and already experienced what was on my horizon. Their stories would have helped me through an incredibly difficult time, but I couldn't find them. I found various websites with scientific breakdowns, but nobody would give it to me straight. So here I am, sharing my story and asking you to do the same. Writing all this out was astonishingly therapeutic and freeing.

So, from one crazy to another: good luck, hang in there, and if your Red feelings get a little out of control, you can buy Dammit Dolls on their website in a variety of colors and patterns. And then, when you're ready…share your story. Share your story for the crazies who are having trouble sorting out their feelings, spend their evenings googling their symptoms and side effects, need a little guidance, or just need to feel like someone else understands. Share your story to free yourself. Share your story on behalf of the crazies who haven't yet found the permission to acknowledge their own story.

With love,
A crazy

Acknowledgments

To Mom, Dad and Brianna: You make life worth living. Thank you for being my rocks, my anchors, and my true north through it all. Thank you for not giving up on me, even when I begged you to.

To Grandma: Even if I didn't want to eat, I couldn't turn down Grandma chicken. Even if I didn't want a hug, I couldn't turn down a Grandma hug. Thank you for always being my loudest and proudest cheerleader, and making Mondays something to look forward to every week.

To Greg and Dr. Montez: You showed me the value of being open, honest, and vulnerable. On behalf of the crazies, thank you for dedicating your careers to helping people like me.

To Kevin and Shannon: No matter the circumstance, you found ways to keep me smiling and laughing. Thank you for letting me be unapologetically myself, and for never once looking at me with pity in your eyes.

To Celina and Isabel: Thank you for treating my words with compassion and tough love. You turned my pages of rambling thoughts and ideas into a book that I couldn't be prouder of.

And finally, to everyone who's ever gotten a Christmas letter from me and said it was funny or that I should try writing something more substantive, thanks for the vote of confidence, however misplaced it might have been. If this book was absolute torture to read, that is entirely your fault for encouraging it.

Made in the USA
Middletown, DE
10 January 2022

58304985R00118